Praise for
Cool Flowers

"Every flower gardener needs this book! Lisa Ziegler's *Cool Flowers* brings to flower gardening a brand new point of view that introduced me to all sorts of possibilities for my floral palette – as a gardener and floral designer. Her valuable tips for success with hardy annuals will extend your garden's blooming season, no matter where you live. If you want to make the most of all seasons in your garden, *Cool Flowers* is a must-have."

~ Debra Prinzing, author of *Slow Flowers* and *The 50 Mile Bouquet*

"*Cool Flowers* is well…really cool. We are all so intent on keeping flowers blooming through the summer and fall that we forget that fall, winter and early spring plantings produce cut flower gardens like none other. Lisa tells us when, where and how to plant, as well as her recommendations for the best flowers for successful cut flowers. Her writing is practical and credible. Give it a read – you will be glad you did."

~ Dr. Allan M. Armitage, Professor Emeritus of Horticulture, University of Georgia, Athens; author of *Armitage's Garden Perennials*; co-founder, Association of Specialty Cut Flower Growers

"Where was this book when I began gardening? Goodness knows, I needed help choosing the best annuals for my garden. Being a flower farmer, Lisa Ziegler knows her hardy annuals, those that can survive winter temperatures and light up the border in spring, and the ones that still perk up the garden come the 4th of July."

~ Dee Nash, author of *The 20-30 Something Garden Guide*

"Who knew growing your favorite old-fashioned hardy annual flowers was so easy? Over the years, flower farmer Lisa Ziegler has figured it out and shares her success. If you love to grow your own flowers, this book will change your gardening forever."

~ Saxon Holt, garden photographer, Photo Botanic

"In user-friendly prose, Lisa Ziegler fills a niche too long neglected...how to grow tough annuals that actually enjoy coloring those challenging gaps between seasons. Follow her sage advice in *Cool Flowers* for glorious blooms, just when your neighbors are dreading their garden's gray winter snooze or last wilting days of summer."

~ Linda Yang, author of *The City Gardener's Handbook*

"Knowledge is the key to success, and *Cool Flowers* is here to help. Finally, here is an easy-to-understand book that explains the difference between hardy and tender annuals (known as half-hardy in the UK) and demystifies the selection and cultivation process. Whether you seek a cutting garden to fill in gaps while shrubs and perennials mature, or simply want to grow easy-care flowers – this is the book you have been waiting for."

~ Karen Chapman, owner of Le Jardinet and co-author of *Fine Foliage*

"Lisa Ziegler takes cut-flower farming to a new level – showcasing her passion for organic gardening and inspiring home gardeners to embrace environmentally friendly living. Her farm is as picturesque as it is productive; it's a gardening landmark in southeastern Virginia. Her new book now allows gardeners everywhere to share in its beauty and purpose."

~ Kathy Van Mullekom, author of the nationally published gardening column "Diggin' In"

"Hardy annual? Half-hardy perennial? The very labels make your eyes glaze over, but Lisa Ziegler has found a way to explain, in simple terms, exactly how to grow these most rewarding of garden flowers. Her writing reminds me of some of the best English garden writers, whose prose came from the heart and whose facts came from experience. "

~ Nancy Ross Hugo, garden writer, naturalist, author of *Seeing Trees* and *Windowsill Art*

"If you have longed to discover the secrets to a truly abundant spring-blooming garden, here's your treasure map! *Cool Flowers* is the book that shows you, step-by-step, how to expand the repertoire of flowers in your gardens. Your heart will sing as you revel in the beauty of growing many of the flowers that bloomed in your grandmothers' gardens."

~ Pamela Arnosky, co-owner of Texas Specialty Cut Flowers/Arnosky Family Farms, Blanco, Texas

Cool FLOWERS

Cool FLOWERS

How to Grow and Enjoy Long-Blooming Hardy Annual Flowers
Using Cool Weather Techniques

Lisa Mason Ziegler

st. lynn's
press

PITTSBURGH

To Kim ~
Souvenirs!
from Mom
X ♡

Cool Flowers
How to Grow and Enjoy Long-Blooming Hardy Annual Flowers Using Cool Weather Techniques

ISBN-13: 978-0-9892688-1-3

Library of Congress Control Number: 2014940985
CIP information available upon request

First Edition, 2014

St. Lynn's Press . POB 18680 . Pittsburgh, PA 15236
412.381.9933 . www.stlynnspress.com

Book design – Holly Rosborough
Editor – Catherine Dees
Editorial Intern – John Gordon

Photo credits courtesy of the following:
page 57, ©Diane Szukovathy; page 58, ©Bertrand; page 115, ©Ford McFall
All other photos ©Suzanne Mason Frye

Printed in Canada
On certified FSC recycled paper using soy-based inks

This title and all of St. Lynn's Press books may be purchased for educational, business, or sales promotional use. For information please write:
Special Markets Department . St. Lynn's Press . POB 18680 . Pittsburgh, PA 15236

10 9 8 7 6 5 4 3

To Mom and Dad.

I pursued my dream because
you said anything is possible.
Thank you.

Table of Contents

A Surprising Discovery

Spring has never been the same since my first season full of snapdragons, bells of Ireland, sweet peas, sweet Williams, and many other beauties. These familiar names may be some of the most admired garden flowers, but, sadly, few people are successfully growing them in their own gardens today. It doesn't have to be that way.

In this book, I share the most surprising discovery I made while pursuing my career as a cut-flower farmer: planting cool-season hardy annuals in the fall and very early spring produces the easiest and earliest-blooming garden ever.

Cool Flowers is all about how and when to plant such flowers – called hardy annuals – so that spring in the garden will be nothing short of sensational. The key is to allow them to get established during cool weather. Plant them in the right spot at the right time, nestle their roots deep into rich organic soil, and stand back. These hardy annuals need little intervention other than having someone gaze on their beauty, or perhaps cut a few for the kitchen table. Once their basic needs are met, this diverse yet easy group of flowers will change spring in your garden forever.

Early summer harvests of hardy annuals.

Success with Hardy Annuals

Hardy annuals are those plants that typically only survive or produce a suitable crop of flowers for one year and are hardy enough to survive cold temperatures of winter. For many regions, these flowers can be planted in the fall to winter-over and bloom in spring – with a repeat planting in very early spring, if desired, to extend the blooming season well into summer.

For the northernmost regions of the country, these are the flowers to plant on the very earliest spring days, long before the last frost date has arrived. These are the flowers you can plant when the gardening bug is itching the most – when the seed catalogs are arriving daily and all you want to do is to get out there and plant *something*.

The truth is, nature stacks the cards for a hardy annual garden (and gardener) to succeed. In fall, winter and early spring, the temperatures are not soaring, so the garden worker is more likely to enjoy the task at hand. The plants are equally happy with the cooler temperatures, which means less stress on the plants. The soil does not dry out as fast, which means fewer watering chores – the rain and snow of fall and winter do the watering for you. Even better, pests and disease are not as active at this time of year.

All of this means success for your garden. Flowers planted during cool weather will become well established and grow a strong root system long before they are expected to

begin performing. These healthy plants will stand on a sturdy foundation that will carry them through spring and into summer, taking on heat, disease, pests and drought with little problem.

Join in on the best-kept secret of gardening – fall, winter, and early spring planting of hardy annuals – for the best garden ever. It will restore your gardening hope and bring spring and summer blooms like you've never seen before. ✄

Lisa

One

HOW FLOWERS CHANGED MY LIFE

My journey to flower farming reads almost like a gardening love story. Growing flowers and living what I consider "the good life" of faith, family and farming leaves little on my want list. It all started because I got the guy and he came with a big garden. Actually, it was far more than just a garden – it was a family homestead that also came with a strong tradition and history of gardening. I was totally smitten from the start by him and this way of life.

Growing up, gardening experiences at my house were all about shady conditions. Our yard came alive with bed after bed of beautiful azaleas and rhododendrons. I remember my dad bringing home the many coffee cans, each with a little baby azalea started by a friend, and our family spending a Saturday planting them until dark. There wasn't much tending required afterwards, just the annual mulching with pine straw that made itself available falling from our pine trees. Easter egg hunts and spring family birthday parties always went hand in hand with the white, pink, red and purple blossoms of azaleas in the background.

As an adult, weekly visits to my grandma's home began to spark my interest in gardening. She shared little bits and pieces of her garden

Steve and Lisa live in Newport News, Virginia, on the Ziegler family homestead with their Golden Retriever, Babs.

with me, and that led me to the library to explore garden books and magazines. I never dreamed I would be so moved and stirred by all the possibilities that a garden could hold. I was wooed by the beautiful photos and wanted a garden of my own.

While exploring my newfound hobby of gardening, I met Steve and asked him out. My interest in him at this point was based solely on his good looks and a friend's suggestion that he was a good one. Little did I know the treasure I would find in both him and his garden.

During our first dinner date, it didn't take long for our conversation to come around to gardening. Living as I was under a deep canopy of oak trees, my little experience had been strictly in shade gardening. Turned out he was quite the vegetable grower. So after our second lunch date, we went by his house to see what he was growing.

Eureka! His little spot of paradise was sitting right smack dab in full sun! I mean no shade in sight – to someone like me who had been searching for a ray of sunshine in her garden, this was incredible. His home was definitely a bachelor's pad, but the garden, oh my goodness – paradise. Most of the property was in beautiful vegetable garden, and there were many plantings around that his grandmother and other family members had started over the years. I just wanted to explore and see what was growing.

Just imagine discovering this spot while living in a city of 180,000 that had little if any undeveloped open land. Steve's home had belonged to his grandparents. It was one of the homes built in the 1930s in what is known as "The Colony" in the Mennonite community located in Newport News, Virginia. The bungalow-type house sat on one and a quarter acres adjoining a 40-acre horse boarding farm. The neighboring fields make this property feel as though you are in the country even though you are in the middle of the city – a treasure in itself.

When I came on the scene, Steve and his family had a large vegetable garden to feed the family in season and for freezing and canning for out-of-season. Grandma Ziegler had planted many hydrangeas, daffodils and camellias on the property over the years. Grandpa Ziegler left his mark also with many fig and pecan trees, grape vines and, most importantly, his years of adding leaf mold to the gardens.

Steve had been living in this place as a bachelor for many years before I came along. In addition to gardening, he had an interest

I now grow the flowers of my dreams because of all the sunshine in Steve's gardens.

in motorcycles. The house apparently was perfect for re-building a 1968 Harley Davidson Chopper in the living room! So glad I missed this. The stories this house could tell: from the babies born to the Brunk family who built the home in the '30s to Harleys roaring up the front steps in the '80s – thank goodness walls can't talk!

Popping the Question

Steve and I hadn't been dating long when I popped the question: "May I do a little gardening at your place?" I just couldn't resist all that sunshine. I could grow... well, I wasn't even sure what I could grow yet, but I was ready to try. He happily replied yes.

So I planted some flowers that I had never before been able to grow. At this point, I just fell in love with the whole gardening life and the one who introduced me to it.

Around here, the story goes that I married Steve for his gardening dowry. Of course, that isn't true! I married Steve because the same things make his heart race as mine: God, family and the love of a garden. However, he did come with a couple of Troy-Bilt tillers, composted land, lots of old hydrangeas, and a dump truck to boot!

Steve and I married in 1995. We had two complete households and gardens. We would ultimately live in his home; however, his place as previously described was a bit of a man cave, so renovations were in order.

We began by packing his house, so he could make the move into my house after the wedding. Next, his house was gutted. The house was taken down to the studs and everything replaced. Keeping it in our regular family style, my brother was the builder and he made the job as painless as possible. The icing on the cake was that my dad custom-made all the trim in the house to replace what was there. Eighteen months later we moved in.

I dug the entire shade garden from my house and brought it with us.

My relocated shade garden that now lives under the tulip magnolia tree that Steve's grandparents planted many years ago. Pictured: hellebores, primroses, bleeding hearts, and cyclamen.

⚬ My First Time with Flowers ⚬

The first year in the Ziegler homestead, I continued the tradition of large vegetable gardens filled with tomatoes, beans, sweet corn, peas, onions, potatoes and all the classics for good eating and storing up. Steve loves growing sweet corn, just like his grandfather did. They loved sharing it with friends and neighbors as much as eating it. I was also busy with projects, putting my own touch on the landscape around our new home, including planting my first 10-foot row of zinnias beside the vegetable garden.

During this time, my grandmother suffered a massive stroke. I was so proud of those zinnias that one day I picked several and took them along on my weekly visit to see her. What a fuss these garden flowers created! I entered the front doors of the nursing home carrying about two dozen zinnias and started down the hall. Folks who had never taken notice before now approached me, saying, "My mother grew those!" or "Zinnias! I had those in my garden." It was one of those moments that makes your heart swell.

By the time I made it to my grandmother's room all the way at the very end of the hall I had a pack of flower garden lovers following me. So began my weekly harvest of zinnias to take on my visit, along with pint mason jars to fill and place on the dining tables for everyone to enjoy as they reminisced.

The experience of harvesting that single row of flowers to take to the nursing home primed me for what was to come. A "big idea" was starting to form in my gardener's brain.

Zinnias are the flower that started it all for me and brought memories to the surface for so many.

I Become a Flower Farmer

During the winter of 1997, I discovered the book *The Flower Farmer*, by Lynn Byczynski. As I began reading this book, everything started falling into place. I was finally in a position that I could explore another career. I had that garden dowry of the necessary equipment, land, even many plants, such as hydrangeas, lily of the valley and peonies, that would complement what I would grow. Steve encouraged me to tackle this full-force. He loved the idea that I might "work the land" as my career, so he was onboard from the get-go.

The blooms from the old hydrangeas Steve's grandmother planted gave my new business venture exactly what it needed – luscious blooms with little effort on my part.

After much head-scratching and nail-biting, I was excited and ready to get started. But it was late summer – what to do? So I hit the books again for a little more research. I found that there were some flowers that could be planted in the fall to bloom the following spring; they were called hardy annuals. It sounded like a great way to start my flower-farming career right then and there, so I bought the recommended seeds and began.

'Chantilly' snapdragons, the earliest snap to bloom in our gardens, often by the first of April.

I planted my first commercial garden that fall – hardy annuals that included snapdragons, sweet peas, sweet William, dill, *Rudbeckia*, and larkspur. When the following March rolled around, I began to start more seeds of the tender season annuals recommended, like zinnias, cockscombs, and lemon basil, to be transplanted out once the soil warmed.

As spring crept in, the fall-planted flowers began to bloom. Steve was so excited for me and asked every day, "Are you taking your flowers down to the florist today?" "Not yet," I said. I was full of reasons. But really, I just had cold feet. Now that my garden flowers were blooming, I began to wonder, would anyone really want them? As the days passed and more and more flowers began to bloom and I didn't make any move to market them, Steve gave me the nudge I needed.

His pep talk was simple. "Take the flowers down there and offer them. If they don't buy them, we just won't ever shop there again." Now I could do that. Something about knowing I wouldn't have to face them again if they turned me down – I married a smart man!

In my gardening ignorance, I never questioned if it would work or not. I never asked myself if my new little plants would survive our winter. Would there actually be flowers come spring? It seemed so simple to me then – the books I was reading said it would work, so I did it. My gift for focusing on the positive rather than the "what-ifs" took me right through that first winter untroubled by doubt. How could I know that this first blind leap of faith would change the course of my life? My fearless plunge into fall planting had a lot to do with the success I now experience as a commercial cut-flower farmer.

The Road to Success

Steve's strategy worked. I felt confident enough to fill the buckets with fragrant sweet pea blooms and mounds of hydrangea blossoms and I headed out. My plan, as suggested in Lynn Byczynski's book, was to offer free flower samples to the customers to show that they are conditioned and of good quality. Well, that plan got blown out of the water soon after my arrival!

At this point, I didn't have a truck, so the flowers were in the back seat of my car. I drove to the shop, hoping that the head designer and

One of my first commercial gardens of hardy annuals.

buyer would be on hand. I walked in with my buckets; he was there, on the phone with his back to me. That was perfect, really. It gave me a moment to collect myself and put my buckets up on the counter. I waited.

While still speaking to the phone customer, he slowly turned to me, and his eyeballs got about the size of tea saucers. His next words were to his phone customer: "Hold just a moment, please," and then to me, "I'll buy them all!"

Then he jumped right back on the phone with the customer. *But wait just a minute*, I was thinking, *I'm here to drop off samples, not to sell them!* Thank goodness he stayed on the phone for a couple of more minutes while I figured out plan B. Once off the phone, he was thrilled with the flowers and the prospect that more were coming. He went on to take me under his wing to help in any way. He showed me how to package, gave me tips, and helped me when I had problems.

My first season went so fast. I realized that I absolutely loved growing masses of flowers. That winter as I planned my garden, it expanded. I needed to also expand my customer base or pretty soon I would have way more cut flowers than customers. It wasn't hard to find more customers. The commercial trade had an appreciation and a demand for locally grown quality flowers. With each passing season, my garden and love of growing flowers increased.

Staple flowers in my spring and early summer gardens: (from left top) yarrow, *Ammi*, black-eyed Susans, feverfew, and bupleurum.

Soon after the beginning of my farm life, my sister, Suzanne Mason Frye, joined me. First it was to help out at the farmer's markets I attended; as my business grew so did her job. She has nurtured the business in those areas she loves – photography and making bouquets. My gardening story wouldn't be complete without saying I would have never come so far or ever reached so high if she hadn't been standing beside me all the way.

Suzanne Mason Frye and Lisa Mason Ziegler

Sixteen years later, our urban farm, now close to three acres in size, has one and a quarter acres in working cutting garden. We continue to sell to the local floral commercial trade, through our on-farm pick-up Garden Share program and Subscription Bouquet drop-offs. In 2012, we also began selling to supermarkets. All of our flowers are grown outdoors in the garden – no greenhouses for us. We follow organic and sustainable practices. Our harvest season is May through October, producing over 10,000 stems of flowers each week.

Maintaining what may be the last working farm in what was once a farming community is an honor that Steve and I treasure. Our commitment to causing no harm and leaving the land better then we found it is our daily goal. Growing cut flowers is the fruit of our labor, but most of all, we just want to be good stewards of all that has been given.

I hope that sharing our experience with growing and loving these amazing flowers will make your own floral journey a wonderful and joyful one.

"The Inn"

A hand-colored photo of the Ziegler family homestead in 1941.

When I moved onto the property in 1996, one of the first jobs I tackled was to clean out The Inn. It looked to me to be the perfect potting shed. Oh, the treasures I found! After relocating all the wonderful family pieces discovered inside, I went to work on the floor. It was covered in old linoleum. What I found when I began pulling it up was incredible. The entire floor was covered in front pages of the newspaper during WWII. The Battle of Midway, and countless other historical news stories, covered the floor. I sat on the floor for hours reading. Unfortunately, they were in such bad shape they couldn't even be lifted off the floor without disintegrating. This lovely building has stood the test of time and today works as a wonderful gardening shed for my flower farm.

The shed pictured on the cover of this book is one of the original buildings on our farm. "The Inn" got its name because it and the other building were used as cottages and temporary homes to many visitors through the years. Farm laborers, travelers and families moving to this community all enjoyed the hospitality of these buildings. Outfitted with potbelly stoves and a string of light bulbs, The Inn had all that was needed to provide for its residents.

Two

THE LIFE OF A HARDY ANNUAL

It's a cold crisp morning in early spring and I'm walking the farm, eyeing the handiwork of fall and late winter. The hard work of preparing soil, starting from seed, planting, and mulching is nothing more than a faded memory as I admire the tall, sturdy snapdragons, their buds ready to burst open. I can hardly take my eyes off the snaps until I notice the sweet pea patch. New little shoots of sweet pea vines are popping through the soil surrounding the baby vine I planted months earlier. The little vine I planted in the fall now appears wind-whipped and exhausted. However, I take heart in knowing that the frostbitten sweet pea vine planted long ago has done its job. It has fostered a root system through the winter that has grown into a well-established and strong foundation for

A spring bouquet of hardy annuals.

this late spring bloomer to soar on. It brings a grin that is hard to lose when I think of those sweet pea vines and snapdragons riding out the coming days, blooming like crazy, even in the midst of heat and humidity.

These early season walks in the garden, allow me to explore and enjoy my garden in a new way. It is still chilly, but warmed by the bright afternoon sunshine. I investigate, pull a weed here and there, and even cut an early-bird bloom to bring in the house. Just a single bloom from the garden in late March and early April takes a place of honor on my desk. Then I carry it to our kitchen table so we can all enjoy the message this bloom is bringing: spring is on its way.

Before I discovered hardy annual gardening, my gardening experiences in late winter and early spring were more about scouring the gardening catalogs as they arrived and just dreaming. Now, it's as if I have been given yet another season in my garden to enjoy.

❧ The Notions of Spring ❧

One of my first hardy annual gardens that included; snapdragons, love-in-a-mist and corn cockle.

The lifecycle of a hardy annual is an oddity to most gardeners. It seems unreasonable to expect anything from seeds or plants put out in the garden when cold weather is just over the horizon, or in early spring while it's still frosty and chilly like winter. It just doesn't make sense. But the truth of the matter – the secret – is that hardy annuals are cut from a different cloth than that of our tender warm-season annuals (the ones we think of when we hear the term "annual"). And that's why we must garden differently if we want these beautiful hardy annual blossoms in our gardens.

At-a-Glance

- **Hardy annuals** live for one year and survive cold temperatures. Many are planted in fall to winter-over and produce blooms the following spring and

summer. These flowers prefer growing in cool conditions.

- **Tender annuals** live for one year and do not survive cold temperatures. These flowers are planted after the threat of frost has passed in spring and the soil has begun to warm. Tender annuals prefer growing in the heat of summer.

Pansies are among the most popular and widely planted spring bloomers. They are hardy annuals. Planting pansies in fall and late winter for the best spring blooms has been common practice for a long time. I like to refer to pansies as the "kissing cousins" to all the other hardy annuals, only related because they enjoy the same type of growing conditions. So, just think of pansies for a moment while we wrap our heads around this concept of hardy annual gardening.

Why is it so tough to grow these spring bloomers? Here's why: in most gardens, spring comes on quickly and moves right into summer. It doesn't hang around long enough to accommodate our natural gardening instinct to plant spring bloomers in... well, spring! We naturally think spring should be like summer. We plant summer bloomers in summer once the warmth starts, and then they grow into valuable members of the long, leisurely summer garden.

Following suit, we storm the garden on the first days of spring with our seed packets, plants and trowels to plant some of the beauties of spring. But it's too late. Spring flowers don't work that way. The window of opportunity has long passed, and our efforts are short-lived and frustrating. We never get the gorgeous display we are promised, because we are planting during the time that this group of flowers is being asked by nature to perform with wild abandon. New little plants just can't do that.

Hardy annuals naturally develop and grow into strong plants when they have opportunity to do it during cool conditions. When these plants get the great start that cool weather provides, their stamina and ability to perform makes you wonder why you didn't think of this sooner. It's all about getting the plants started and established during their preferred growing conditions. Once they are well established, hardy annuals seem to look adversity in the face and bloom even more. What I said in the introduction bears repeating: plant them in the right spot, at the right time, nestle their roots deep into rich organic soil, and stand back.

What is a Hardy Annual?

The term hardy annual indicates a plant that typically lives for one year and doesn't just survive the cold, but thrives under cooler temperatures. Both plants and seeds can be planted in the fall, winter and/or early spring depending on your region. In a large portion of the country, hardy annuals can be fall-planted to winter-over as immature plants. This allows them to establish an incredibly strong root system that gives the earliest possible blooms in spring and keeps them performing well into warm and hot weather. In more northern zones where there are frigid conditions or heavy snow loads, these flowers can be planted in the very early spring while waiting for warm temperatures to arrive. For those who plant in the fall, a repeat planting in very early spring can extend the blooming season; we do this with excellent results on our farm here in southeast Virginia.

As a general guide, hardy annuals can be planted 6-8 weeks before the first frost of fall, to winter-over as an immature plant, and/or planted 6-8 weeks before your last frost in spring. When you plant depends on where your garden falls on the hardiness zone map (page 138). Getting this better understanding of what makes hardy annuals tick will help you to tweak these guidelines even more to suit your garden.

I encourage you to be bold and experiment with flowers that may thrive just outside of your zone; sometimes those results are the sweetest of all.

The life cycle. The hardy annual's natural life cycle is to go from seed into making seed in the span of one year. The annual plant's whole purpose in life is to grow into a plant to produce flowers that will produce seeds – and then die. The confusion with hardy annuals comes because their year of life follows a different calendar than we are accustomed too. They begin life from a seed in the fall, then winter-over as a young plant, becoming well established so that when spring arrives, they quickly grow into a robust plant. Their life cycle continues as they bloom, make seed, and die.

This is why, once your plants start producing flowers in spring, you have a choice to make.

Bachelor buttons holding their own as the snow cover melts away providing a deep slow watering.

On the one hand, you can remove the flowers as they bloom by either harvesting them for cut flowers or dead-heading once they begin to fade. This way, you will keep your plant producing more and more flowers in an effort to get those seeds made. However, if you choose to leave the faded and dead flower heads in the garden, they will develop into seeds. At that point, the blooming will cease because the plant believes its job is done and it's time to die.

Knowing what the hardy annual is programmed to do can help you get the most from your plants in a profusion of continuing blooms. Here on our farm, we cut the flowers weekly to have as fresh cut flowers. This routine harvest keeps most of the plants blooming long after their expected time. Your course of action will depend on the purpose of your garden. Is it a cutting garden, a container for display, a landscape to enjoy, or a bed to attract birds and pollinators?

Other Plants You Can Grow as Hardy Annuals

Delphinium are a perennial in the north, but gardeners in the lower half of the country can grow them as hardy annuals with great success.

In this book you will also learn about some plants known as *perennials* and *biennials* that can function better in some gardens as hardy annuals. Doing so brings satisfaction and success where it may not have been possible before. Growing conditions make some perennials almost impossible to maintain year-round. But they may be perfect additions to the garden when treated as a hardy annual. A great example of this is the delphinium. In the northern regions, delphiniums grow into amazing plants that return year after year. In other parts of the country, we can grow fabulous delphiniums by treating them as a hardy annual. The heat and humidity of our late summers weaken the delphinium so that they fall victim to disease and pests. It is liberating to the gardener to know when to plant these flowers so they can perform at their best. The gardener can work with nature to plant in the fall, look forward to a strong performance in spring and summer and then, when late summer arrives, accept their ultimate demise. New seedlings can be planted in fall for the next season.

Another time that we treat a perennial as a hardy annual is when it is not a particularly strong or long-lived plant. Such plants are often called a *half-hardy perennial*. Feverfew follows this habit, a great

'Virgo" feverfew is my favorite because of its tight cluster of button blooms.

garden plant that flowers from seed the first year. In subsequent years, it either disappears or loses its attractiveness in the garden. To prevent suffering an untimely loss or experiencing a hole in the garden, we grow feverfew as a hardy annual, replanting yearly in the fall for a profusion of button blooms every spring.

A biennial such as foxglove can also be grown as a hardy annual. This allows you to eliminate much of the growing time normally spent in tending and caring for a plant that will not bloom until the following year. Biennials are not as widely grown because of this

long time-lapse to get results. Traditional seeds are sown in late spring. The plant must be tended all summer and into fall to have it go through winter and produce blooms the following spring.

But growing foxglove as a hardy annual is different. You start plants from seed in late summer, allowing the immature plant to winter-over, and then watch the plant bloom the following spring. This way, you have eliminated months of plant care during the heat and possible droughts of summer.

Easy to Get Started

Many hardy annuals prefer to have their seeds cast directly in the garden. The fall and early spring seasons often tend to our seeds better than we do. This is the best time to get acquainted with planting seeds in the garden, because it is the most forgiving time. There is a little rain and snow just when it is needed, along with cooler night temperatures and some warm days. All of this makes perfect growing conditions for our seeds. Add to this the benefit of the winter rains and snows, and they will thrive with little attention from the gardener until it's time to bloom. Some will cast their own seeds in the garden to return year after year. Once your plants begin to cast their own seeds, you can take your cues from Mother Nature when to plant. Some of the greatest lessons learned have come from mimicking what nature does, and when.

The seeds of many hardy annuals can also be easily started indoors. It is sometimes more practical to do this and then move the transplants into the garden. Because mulching can be done right away when planting, it reduces the need for weed prevention chores and can widen the window of times to plant. A nice bonus to starting indoors is the comfort of the gardener on hot summer or cold winter days. In the dog days of late summer, I thoroughly enjoy heading indoors to start seeds for fall planting.

Bells of Ireland baby plants that wintered over. I planted their seeds directly in the garden the previous fall.

In my experience, one of the greatest struggles of late winter is to resist starting tender annuals such as zinnias and sunflowers too soon. These warm season plants become overgrown and unhappy waiting for the soil to warm for the proper planting time. Starting hardy annual seeds to be planted into cool soil fills that urge perfectly, and helps the gardener wait until the proper time to start tender annuals.

On a visit to my friend Dave Dowling's flower farm, Suzanne and I discovered these gorgeous delphiniums 'Pacific Giants'.

Growing hardy annuals is especially appealing because you prepare and plant them at a time when little else is going on in the garden. Preparing the garden becomes a plea-sure as you tackle the task during the fall when cool nights and shorter days have arrived. If you are planting both in the fall and in early spring, the soil should be prepared in fall. Winter rains and snow make it difficult to find a dry spell to dig in the garden for early spring planting.

A Haven for Pollinators

With your hardy annual garden you're going to notice the vast number of early season "good bugs" buzzing around. This would include native bees and many other pollinators. Because there are so few sources of nectar and pollen this early in the season, hardy annuals really provide for these guys when they need it most. This also gives my garden an early start on building the community of beneficial insects that are essential to our organic gardening success. While many gardeners are aware of the benefits of the most popular beneficial insect, the ladybugs, there is a whole army of others that help our gardens as well. Many of these beneficial insects are searching for food and a place to live and raise babies in spring. A garden planted in fall, winter and/or early spring is a perfect fit for them.

Watching and Waiting

The anticipation I experience waiting for this garden to pop full of blooms during the winter and early spring compares to little else. All winter I watch from the window, wondering about those little plants I planted in fall. Will they survive the whipping winds and below-freezing temperatures? The snow? Yes, they do survive, they really do. This scenario plays out in my mind every year. Perhaps the scariest thing I do in January is to go out and take a closer look just to see what is going on in this garden. It's always the same; I am met with frozen, tattered plants that look like they will never live to produce a bloom. Panic sets in. Then I remind myself that the most valuable part of the plant at this time of year is the root stretching and going deep underground, hiding away snuggled in rich soil and protected with mulch. My heart leaps for joy every year when I see the first little green shoot pushing up next to that tattered plant.

The blooms of this black-eyed Susan (*Rudbeckia* 'Indian Summer') are often larger than your hand.

Pincushion Flowers

There are so many aspects of a hardy annual garden that are empowering to gardeners: you plant when little else is going on in the garden; it is cooler; rain is more frequent, eliminating watering chores; and the act of fall planting introduces a new feeling of anticipation for spring. Waiting for this group of flowers to jump into action in spring is so exciting. I find myself snooping around the garden just looking, wondering and waiting. I could stay out there for days cuddling these plants – even though they don't require it! I know that for the rest of the winter they are ready and waiting to perform for me. That is just one of the many reasons I love to garden.

Once you understand this fascinating, easy, and beautiful group of flowers, I think you will be hooked too.

Three

WHEN TO PLANT: FOLLOWING MOTHER NATURE'S CALENDAR

When it comes to hardy annual gardening, nothing has a greater impact on success than the timing of planting. With dismal results, many of us have been planting hardy annuals just at the very time when most of them should be bursting into bloom. I think the confusion around when to plant is deeply rooted in the word "annual," because we commonly associate it with flowers we plant in spring to bloom through the summer – the tender annuals. How did we lose our understanding of hardy annual flowers and when they should be planted?

One of the most fragrant and beautiful sweet peas – 'High Scent'.

A Rekindled Concept

It used to be common practice to include hardy annuals in the garden. In the 1950s, most homes had a vegetable garden out of necessity. The mother of the house usually tended the garden and she often indulged her fancy for flowers as well. This close connection had the

A favorite on our farm for its large blossoms, sweet pea 'Geranium Pink'.

gardeners so in tune with the garden that they planted and reaped in almost every season.

On the kitchen bookshelf next to the *Betty Crocker Picture Cookbook*, you would find the *Better Homes and Gardens Garden Book* (published 1951). Both were homemaking staples of the day. The garden book featured advice on planting hardy annuals in the fall, winter and early spring. Obviously, the cool-season planting I describe is not a new concept at all – it is merely being rekindled.

This strong tradition of a home garden diminished over the intervening decades as supermarkets began offering more and more fresh vegetables, making it unnecessary to "grow your own." Lost along with the homegrown vegetables was that little flower garden and our knowledge of how to grow and tend it.

Today, with the revival of the home garden, hardy annuals are beginning to show up again in landscapes. They are rejoining the vegetable garden and the cutting garden. The romance of these old-fashioned favorites stirs the memories of yesteryear.

Over the years, when I brought my sweet peas to sell at a local farmer's market, I knew exactly what to expect. It never failed that a customer would come along and lift one of our sweetie bouquets to her nose. She would close her eyes, breathing in the fragrance, and say, "Ahh…my grandmother always grew sweet peas. I haven't thought of that fence of flowers or that fragrance in years!"

So while new to us, planting in what might seem like an awkward season is really just a discovery of something old made new again.

Planting Time Options

There are hardy annuals suitable to plant in every garden, each with its own set of rewards. Gardeners just have to find where their gardens fit the cycle. Those gardening in the lower half of the 48 states enjoy the most flexibility in planting times, while those in the north, with colder winters and cooler summers, benefit from blooms lingering longer into summer.

When you plant will depend on where your garden in located on the hardiness zone map. To learn what "planting time" options you have, first find where your garden falls on the hardiness zone map found on page 138. The next necessary step is to find the expected first frost date in fall and the last frost date in spring for your area. The local Cooperative Extension office will be able to provide this information.*

Once armed with the hardiness zone and expected frost dates, you can easily make a plan and mark a calendar with your fall, winter, and/or spring "planting time" options.

Planting window timelines:

- Fall planting is 6-8 weeks before your first frost date.
- Winter planting is when ground is not frozen.
- Early spring planting is 6-8 weeks before your last frost date.

To locate the Cooperative Extension office near you, visit http://www.csrees.usda.gov/Extension/

Sweet Peas

A great way to get started is to choose flowers that are winter hardy in your winter hardiness zone. Chapter 5, "Flower-by-Flower," includes the winter hardiness for each flower. So, once you know your hardiness zone, you can flip through and find flowers that will survive with as little fanfare as possible in your zone.

Marking the Calendar

The process of incorporating hardy annuals into my garden became much clearer when I notated all the key dates on our family's day-to-day calendar, the one I look at every single day. Because the seed-starting and planting are at non-traditional gardening times, I needed a reminder while I was retraining my automatic gardening memory. Seeing when to do what at a glance really helped.

Helpful dates to mark:

- First frost in fall
- Last frost in spring
- Count back 8 weeks from both of these dates to find planting dates.
- Count back from planting dates for indoor seed starting dates.

Fall

The optimal time for fall planting is 6-8 weeks before your first frost date. Treat this time frame as a guide, not an absolute. I have fudged by a few weeks both early and late with great success. As summer moves into fall and then into winter, growing conditions are ideal for planting seeds and transplants: nighttime temperatures start to fall, the days are not heating up as intensely, and rain comes more frequently.

The timeline you set up for getting started will depend on whether you are planting seeds directly in the garden or starting seeds indoors to plant transplants. The preferred method of seed starting is listed for each flower in Chapter 5.

Planting seeds directly in the garden. This method requires advance planning in order to have the necessary seeds on hand at the proper planting time. Growing conditions are excellent for sprouting hardy annual seeds in the garden in fall. Planting while the days are still warm speeds germination. If seeds are planted later and do not receive the necessary warmth to trigger sprouting in fall, they will lie dormant until those conditions are favorable again. The drawback to this method is that your plants will not have spent the winter developing the

Sweet William 'Sweet" is amongst the very first bloomers in our spring garden.

29

beneficial strong root system. To make matters worse, cool-season weeds will quickly fill in where there are no plants. Ideally, the goal is to plant the seeds with enough time for them to sprout and grow into a small plant, so they can be mulched and then put to bed for the winter.

'Rocket' snapdragons are the hardiest and are the last snap variety to start to bloom in my garden.

Starting seeds indoors. You will need to start early enough to have a suitable-size plant at the proper planting time. The time lapse from planting a seed to a suitable plant size varies between varieties. Because I prefer to have a larger transplant going into winter, I start all seeds indoors 6-8 weeks before the planting time outdoors, except where I have noted on specific flowers. The window for getting seeds started indoors for fall planting puts the task right in the heat of summer – when it is a treat to have an indoor gardening project!

Go with fall if possible!

What I have experienced and heard from other growers is that whenever you have the option to plant hardy annuals in the fall versus early spring, go with fall. The strength and quality of young plants that have spent all winter building a deep and strong root system are unrivaled by their counterparts planted in early spring. The carefree nature of these well-established plants requires little (if any) intervention from the gardener. Coupled with pleasant planting conditions in the fall, this creates a win-win situation for the gardener.

While I plant many in the fall, I also repeat that same planting in very early spring in an effort to extend our season of bloom. This spring planting will typically begin to bloom when the fall planting of the same flower starts into its decline. What I have learned from this is that the fall-planted plants bloom earlier, produce more and taller stems, and continue blooming longer into the heat and humidity of summer. The early spring planting is certainly a worthy garden member; it just stars a little later and doesn't perform to the level of a fall planting. So, choose fall planting if it is an option – the benefits are many.

Winter

Winter planting is an option in frost-free regions of the Deep South or in gardens where the ground doesn't freeze in winter. The way to succeed with winter planting is to prepare the soil in the fall and have it ready and waiting for planting time. One of the benefits of winter for the hardy annuals is the consistent moisture – but this constant moisture is also what makes it next to impossible to prepare soil in winter. I like to prepare the area in fall and then cover with mulch to prevent winter weeds and to keep the soil temperature more stable. When it is time to plant during winter, I pull back the mulch to plant seeds directly, or plant transplants right through the mulch.

A bed of love-in-a-mist ready to burst into bloom.

Planting seeds directly in the garden. Seeds planted in the dead of winter will most often lie dormant until spring. If you do this, I would pay close attention to marking this planting with plant markers to stir your memory come spring, when they will sprout amongst all the spring weeds.

Starting seeds indoors. This can be done any time for later transplant in the garden. Providing added protection, like a row cover, will enhance winter growth both above and below ground level.

Early Spring

The optimum time for early spring planting is 6-8 weeks before your last frost date. In early spring, hardy annuals are the seeds and plants to lay our hands on when we have the itch to garden. We can turn to this family of plants as the gardening catalogs begin to arrive, tempting us to bolt outdoors and plant.

Early spring is the time to plant those flowers that are not winter hardy in your zone – you simply plant them in early spring after the worst of winter has passed. I plant all the flowers that won't survive our winters and many of the same ones I planted in fall, in an effort to extend their bloom time. For best results and because of those early spring showers, it is necessary to prepare the soil the previous fall for an early spring planting. It can be nearly impossible to find a window of dry soil conditions during spring.

Engaging your garden in early spring can be an exciting time. Exploring among your plantings old and new will reveal surprises you never imagined.

The timeline you set up for getting started will depend on whether you are planting seeds directly in the garden or starting seeds indoors to plant transplants. See Chapter 5 for the preferred method of seed starting for your flowers.

Planting seeds directly in the garden. Seed planting in early spring is so rewarding! Warming temperatures and frequent rains result in quick germination. Unfortunately, the unwanted weeds appreciate those very same conditions so they too are on the fast track to sprouting and growing. See Chapter 6 for how to prevent weeds from becoming a problem when planting seeds directly in the garden. I cover all of our new plantings with a row cover for 2-3 weeks to provide added protection from the elements. I find row cover especially valuable in early spring to protect from strong winds and an increasing population of hungry birds present in the garden eager for seeds.

Starting seeds indoors. While still in the deep throes of winter, this is a restorative gardening job that many enjoy immensely. To have seeds sprouting and growing indoors during the short days of winter really brings spring anticipation on in a new way. It's fun to start seeds during or just following the holidays, but unless you plan ahead, you may find yourself without the seeds you need on hand for this early task.

Feverfew

It's a good idea to order all your seeds in fall or early winter. You don't want to have to delay your seed starting for lack of seeds. When spring arrives, you will only reap the benefits of a well-established plant if you have started your seeds at the right time. (Seed ordering is a helpful date to mark on the calendar.)

While the growth rate varies between varieties, 6-8 weeks before the planting outdoor date is a good guide to start seeds. Having bigger transplants is not as critical in spring, because plants will grow more rapidly than their fall and winter counterparts when planted in the garden at that time.

Take that Leap of Faith and Plant!

As I discovered this old-and-made-new-again way of gardening, I felt as though I was stumbling along not knowing how the journey would turn out. I had no idea how rewarding it would be. Looking back now, my experience with the hardy annual garden I planted that first fall started what has now snowballed into this gardening good life I love and feel called to.

I took the leap of faith and planted. Then followed weeks of standing at the chilly wintery window... wondering. At last, the fabulous surprise when the plants survived winter to bloom in spring! That is how this new chapter opened in the life of my garden.

Because of hardy annuals, I now feel as though I have my finger on the pulse of my garden. Instead of showing up in the garden in spring when the daffodils are opening, I am out there rooting around most any time of year, witnessing as things are developing. I don't wait to discover the end result in spring. I am constantly on the lookout for the seedlings of self-sowing flowers that have begun to germinate on their own. You can experience this as early as your second year of hardy annual gardening with the self-sowers showing themselves at their optimal time for your garden.

When you are in tune with your garden, you will find that Mother Nature is sending out all kinds of messages. Mimicking nature by following her clues makes gardening much simpler and more successful – like her timing of self-sowers. You just have to get it started by being willing to plant and become a part of it all.

My willingness to risk failure has brought about much success in my garden. After experiencing some success with hardy annuals, perhaps you will tiptoe into planting flowers that survive the zone just south of you. You can always tweak your planting conditions to create a more hospitable microclimate. Some of our most spectacular spring flowers are those I had to test the waters with. Be bold and dare to succeed!

Four

ACHIEVING HEALTHY SOIL: THE FOUNDATION OF YOUR GARDEN

❧

Think of gardening, and the mind tends to flash to the glossy photos in seed catalogs – radiant blossoms and succulent vegetables in every hue of the rainbow. While these are certainly the ultimate goal (or maybe just pie in the sky) they tell you nothing about what gardening really is. The definition of gardening is the activity of tending and cultivating a garden, especially as a pastime. It's this tending and cultivating that not only makes a garden near and dear to our hearts, but it is the simple secret to success. In fact, the secret is so simple that most people miss it.

Throughout the past sixty years or so, the concept of the garden has come and gone, only to return recently to the home landscape. But it would appear that this all-important tending and cultivating has been lost along the way. (Yet another practice of yesteryear lost for us to rediscover.) Once a part of daily living, gardening has become a weekend activity for many of us. These less frequent but more intense garden encounters are now rolled into a Saturday morning that can overwhelm the want-to-be gardener. It's not so much a daily tending and cultivating anymore – just a long list of chores that must be done. The joy of the process is lost to the hustle and the weeds.

I was once one of those overwhelmed want-to-be gardeners. I had grand visions of a beautiful landscape skirting my home with cutting and vegetable gardens in the backyard that would somehow produce abundance whenever I needed it. These visions of grandeur led me to becoming a slave to never-ending maintenance and an out-of-control chore list.

This all changed when I learned that there is more to a garden than just a pretty zinnia or a juicy red tomato. It was the tending and cultivating part I had been missing. Of course I was "preparing soil" when I planted, and I was pulling weeds when they grew. But I did those things because I thought that is what it took to get the bounty – not because it was the lifeline of my garden.

When Your Soil is Weakened

The aha! moment came when I finally understood that the soil is literally the foundation of the garden, the rock that it stands on. When soil is healthy, full of life and open for roots and all good things to flow through, your plants naturally grow into robust plants and are resistant to disease and pests. When the soil is "dead," your plants suffer by being puny and riddled with pests and diseases. Dead soil results from a lack of organic matter that sustains life. The repetitive use of synthetic fertilizers and other chemicals damages soil health and creates garden soil that is a desert.

Compare your home and its foundation with the garden and its soil, and you will see the likenesses. If the foundation has cracks, holes and weak spots, your home will be vulnerable to all kinds of problems. Your walls will crack, the floors will sag, and perhaps vermin will set up housekeeping under the house. The very same is true in your garden.

When the soil of your garden is weak, dead and compacted, your garden is vulnerable to pests, disease and weeds. In order to just barely survive, the garden will need a lot of assistance from you, and that means hard work. This creates a cycle for the gardener of continuously focusing on reviving plants rather than encouraging a thriving plant with enhanced growing conditions.

When we enhance and assist nature in place of trying to overpower it, gardening actually becomes easier. I have lived and experienced it. With each passing year, as my garden becomes more and more self-sustaining, it relies less and less on me for life.

This chapter will outline the easy steps to begin, and continue, restoring the natural order of your garden. Tending thriving, healthy plants that need little help from you can be simple, and it all starts with the soil. Once you start down this path, you will suddenly realize that you are truly tending and cultivating. You will see that gardening has indeed become the pastime of your heart's desire.

Providing Favorable Conditions

Hardy annuals are planted during cool to cold weather. During those times, detrimental conditions tend to persist and are difficult to correct after the fact. Choosing a location with wind and drainage in mind can prevent many problems.

Drainage. If your site has poor drainage and it is a very wet fall, winter and spring, there is little you can do to dry out the site and save the soggy roots. Providing an avenue in advance for the water to drain away from the roots will prevent winter root or crown rot. In addition to choosing a site that isn't soggy, follow the steps on pages 40-42 to create a raised bed and open the subsoil for better drainage.

Wind. A windy winter site can dehydrate plants and cause constant stress unnecessarily. For best results, locate a site in your yard that offers some wind protection.

A raised bed provides excellent drainage for 'Rocket' Snapdragons.

This is called a *microclimate*. A microclimate is a spot where conditions are different from the surrounding area. If you walk your yard with the intention of seeking out your micro-climates, they will make themselves apparent after a few trips around at different times of day.

Location and microclimates. The best microclimates are naturally occurring, but you can also create them. A naturally-occurring microclimate might be a bed located on the southeast side of your house. It is protected from wind and receives the early morning sun when temperatures are at their lowest. This same bed on the opposite side of the house might be shaded until mid-morning and receive the constant west wind. If you were a plant that is trying to live through cold frosty times in a garden, which location would you choose? Just a little thought to where you plant can go a long way in your garden success.

Don't let the lack of the perfect location stop you from including hardy annuals in your garden. In fact, where I farm there are cold, rolling winds almost non-stop all winter. We grow hardy annuals in spite of this wind – we just create our own microclimate. See Chapter 7 for how to create a microclimate.

Steps to determine a microclimate and available sunlight:

1. For best results, spend one full day at home from sunrise to sunset.

2. On paper, number and indicate what areas you suspect are microclimates in your yard.

3. A little after sunrise, walk the yard and observe each area. Windy? Sun or shade? Make notes on the paper about the time and what you found in each area.

4. Repeat this all day every hour. As a reminder, set a timer for 1 hour each time you return indoors.

5. At the end of the day, tabulate your results.

6. Full sun is 6-8 hours in an area, part sun is 4-6 hours, and shade is considered 4 or less hours.*

7. The most desirable microclimates would be those with the least amount of wind.

Other factors should be considered, depending on the time of year, like deciduous trees that have dropped or will drop their leaves.

When to Prepare the Soil

If you are planting hardy annuals in winter and early spring, it is best to prepare the site in the preceding fall. Soil conditions are more favorable in fall – not water-logged from winter rains and snow. This time of resting before planting will also allow for the soil to mellow nicely after incorporating organic matter and organic fertilizer. To prevent winter weeds from sprouting and growing in the newly prepared site, mulch immediately following preparation. See Chapter 8 for more on weed prevention.

Getting Your Garden Soil Going

Most everyone I have the "soil conversation" with feels like they have the worst soil ever and that their garden is doomed. The truth and good news is that great soil is a result of working at it a little bit at a time over the life of your garden. Great soil is made, not born.

The goals of the following steps are to open the soil as deeply as possible to improve drainage and to crack open the hard subsoil. This will allow plant roots to go deep to seek out water and nutrients you don't have to provide. All of the organic matter incorporated will feed and restore microorganisms in the soil, increase moisture retention and improve overall health in the soil.

What are microorganisms and why are they so important?

Microorganisms are the underground superstars in every thriving organic garden. On our farm, we try to give them everything they need to survive and reproduce. They are the good guys that run around underground gobbling up the organic matter you add to the soil. They are beneficial because they eat bad guys like harmful nematodes in the garden soil and actually create nutrition for your plants when they die. The more good microorganisms present in your soil, the less bad ones will be there. Repetitive use of synthetic fertilizers and chemicals harms and kills these good microorganisms.

How to Get the Soil Started in a Bed:

What you'll need:

Wheelbarrow

Digging tools (we use a border spade and fork)

Dry organic fertilizer

Organic compost (enough to cover the area with 5-6 inches by the time it is complete)

1. Before beginning, remove all vegetation from the bed.
2. Stand on the long side of the bed at the left end with the wheelbarrow at your left.
3. Using the spade, push the blade (jump on it!) into the ground as deeply as you can with no need to go beyond 4-6 inches.

Lift the soil out and place it in the wheelbarrow. Continue to lift the soil in this manner across the width of the bed (3 feet).

4. Move to the right and lift the next row of soil out and place in wheelbarrow.
5. The hole you have made has revealed the *subsoil.* Using the fork, place it on the subsoil and again push (jump on it!), driving it as deeply as possible. Then rock the fork handle back and forth to crack and open the earth.

6. Remove the fork and move it a couple of inches and repeat. Make cracks and holes through the exposed subsoil.
7. Place 2-4 inches of compost on the subsoil, covering the holes and cracks.

8. Using the border spade, move to the right and again remove two rows of soil, but instead of placing in the wheelbarrow, place it on top of the layer of compost you just added.

9. Continue down the bed until you reach the end.

10. At the end of the bed, make your holes and cracks with the fork and add compost. Then move the wheelbarrow down the bed's length and dump the soil evenly.

11. Top the entire bed with 2-4 inches of compost and add the dry organic fertilizer according to instructions.

12. Using the border fork, mix together, breaking up any large lumps.

you have opened the earth 10-14 inches below the soil level. Now your plants' roots (along with all the microorganisms and other beneficial creatures) have 14-22 inches of loose, rich soil to grow deep and wide into. The end result? A stronger and more robust plant that will fight off disease and pests, grow taller and require less water.

This process will give you a bed raised 4-8 inches from its starting level because of adding organic matter and loosening the soil – plus,

Note: avoid stepping into the bed to crush all those openings you just created in the soil. This is why I prefer 3-foot-wide and narrower beds – I can reach to the middle from the sides.

❧ Feeding the Soil for Life ☙

After a season of growing plants in a healthy bed of soil, you will be eager to maintain and enhance the bed by feeding it. To do so, simply pull the spent flowers from the bed, roots and all. Do this without stepping on the bed, and add the spent plants to your compost heap.

Before the next planting, repeat steps 11 and 12, above. The bed will be ready for planting. Repeating these two steps at each replant will create a garden bed that becomes more self-sustaining with each passing year.

This process is what I call "feeding the soil." Continue to feed your soil for life with organic matter.

Important: do an annual checkup on your soil; submit a soil test to see if all is well. Seek out laboratories that offer organic solutions for any deficiencies found in your soil.* Gardening without soil testing is like gardening in the dark.

Contact your local Cooperative Extension office for where to send soil for testing.

Feeding the Soil in a Permanent Planting

Feeding the soil also benefits more permanent plantings of trees, shrubs, and perennials. Using a border fork, go throughout the bed, but be careful to avoid the area within the drip line of plants. The drip line is the area of ground from the center stem to the tip of the stem. Push the fork in deeply and rock it to make holes and cracks, then remove, move a few inches and repeat. Apply 1 inch of compost to the bed. Decorative mulch can be applied on top of compost for aesthetics. Doing this each year will improve the quality of the soil and moisture retention.

Container Potting Mix

What I have learned about container gardening over the years is that a bigger container is definitely better than smaller. The larger the container, the more room roots have to grow. You will have to water less often because of the larger mass of soil. I like to recycle my potting soil and actually make it better with each passing year, much like my garden – with one exception. It doesn't happen often, but if I have a pot that was home to a plant with some disease or pest issue, I dump that soil in the compost heap in place of mixing for repotting.

A potted white pansy will brighten any spot.

So here are the steps to recycle and rejuvenate your potting soil:

What you'll need:
Wheelbarrow
Compost
Dry organic fertilizer
Coco fiber or peat moss

1. Collect all your containers and dump the old potting mix in the wheelbarrow.
2. Remove any plant debris and break up the soil.
3. Mix 2 parts old soil, 1 part compost and 1 part coco fiber or peat moss.
4. Add organic fertilizer according to instructions.
5. Your fresh potting soil is ready to use.

Any excess potting mix can be stored in a container that is not airtight. You can also dump any extra into your garden.

The Organic Golden Rule

Plant the right plant – sun lovers in sun, shade lovers in shade, etc.

At the right time – planting hardy annuals in cool seasons, etc.

In the right place – in healthy soil and favorable conditions.

Follow the rules to organic gardening success. Plants literally can't help themselves but to thrive when you provide what they need. It really is that simple.

Five

FLOWER-BY-FLOWER

So, who are these flowers that reward us so beautifully when we plant them in cool conditions? First, you must know that the flowers in this chapter are simply my favorites as of today – I am sure that as I continue to experiment with others there will be more flowers to add to this group of easy-keeper, cool-season lovers.

These 30 flowers are my favorites for different reasons. Some, for their beautiful display in the garden, others because I can't imagine a garden bouquet without them, and then some I plant because they are such worthy garden members.

It's those worthy flowers that sometimes need a little more highlighting because the showboats and those commonly seen in fresh flower bouquets have already endeared themselves to the gardener. Don't underestimate the beauty, the need and usefulness of the less-than-eye-popping flowers, because they each have a role. It may be filling in the spaces of the garden between the colorful showboats or in a bouquet adding texture and interest. Or most importantly, they could be one of those early bloomers that provide crucial habitat and food for pollinators. Consider each one of these flowers as a potential for your garden, while perhaps for different reasons.

As you consider how these flowers might fit into your garden, keep in mind that the key to a carefree garden is to give the plants the longest possible time to get established before they must grow, bloom and face adverse conditions like heat and humidity. To maximize this benefit, always plant as early as possible for your zone. As I mentioned earlier in these pages, sometimes it's good to step outside of rigid zone limits. If you'd love to grow one of these plants in fall, but it's only winter hardy to one zone south of you, go ahead and try it anyway – taking a chance sometimes works and it reaps the greatest reward.

Lisianthus

Guide to the Flower-by-Flower Pages

In this chapter, every flower profile will include quick-reference information about sun requirements, zone range, height, spacing in the garden, deer resistance, reseeding potential, and container use.

For each flower, I give the method or methods for starting the plant from seed (sow outdoors or sow indoors). If two methods are indicated for a given flower, the one listed first is the preferred one. I also indicate whether the just-sown seed should be covered with a thin layer of soil or left uncovered; and I show the number of days to sprout and any special handling that is needed. Be aware that a variation in growing conditions (moisture and temperature) can result in more days to sprout.

Seed Starting Key
(for more complete information about starting seeds, see Chapter 6)

Sow outdoors, do not cover
Plant seeds directly in the garden. Sprinkle onto the soil and then gently firm in with the press of your hand; do not push soil on top of seeds. Light aids in sprouting. Water the seeds in well and keep moist until sprouting.

Sow outdoors, do cover
Plant seeds directly in the garden. Sprinkle onto the soil and cover with ¼-inch of soil. Darkness aids in germination. Gently firm in with the press of your hand. Water the seeds in well and keep moist until sprouting.

Sow indoors, do not cover
Start seeds indoors. Place seed firmly on the surface and do not cover with soil. Light aids in sprouting. Seeds sprout indoors with a soil temperature of 65-75 degrees. Keep soil moist until sprouting, allowing to dry slightly between waterings.

Sow indoors, do cover
Start seeds indoors. Place seed firmly on the surface and cover with ¼-inch of soil. Darkness aids in sprouting. Seeds sprout indoors with a soil temperature of 65-75 degrees. Keep soil moist until sprouting, allowing to dry slightly between waterings.

Note: You will see that I often suggest using a row cover or support netting to help a plant to do its best. Appendix C provides information about these useful garden items, along with sources for purchasing them.

Ammi § *Ammi majus and Ammi visnaga*

The white, lacy blooms of the *Ammi* family are admired in the garden and in bouquets for their long lasting flowers. Often called bishop's flower, they are mirror images of the naturalized wild carrot known as Queen Anne's lace. Although the blooms are similar among the members of this family, the foliage varies from one variety to another. We love and grow them all! Beneficial insects, such as ladybugs and parasitic wasps, are especially attracted to the clusters of tiny florets that make up these large, flat blooms.

FACTS TO GROW ON:

Part to full sun: 4-8 hours
Start from seed: Sow indoors, do not cover; or sow outdoors, do not cover; sprouting in 7-14 days
Zone: Winter hardy to zone 7
Height: 36" - 48"
Spacing: Landscape 12"; Cutting 9"
Deer resistance: Good
Reseeding potential: Excellent
Container use: Poor, not recommended

TIPS TO FOR EASY SUCCESS:

Leaving a few flower heads on the plants in the garden after they have faded will allow them to produce seeds that will naturally scatter in your garden. These tall flowers have large flower heads and will benefit from flower support netting to prevent tumbling during rainstorms.

WINTER STRATEGIES:

Covering with a single layer of floating row cover provides enough protection to result in a more robust plant and earlier blooms than those left uncovered.

KEEP THE BLOOMS COMING:

Leaving some of the faded heads in the garden will provide habitat and food for pollinators.

For Cut Flowers: Make the first cut of the central stem at almost ground level, just above the lowest two to three side shoots. Side shoots will continue to mature and develop branching after the central stem is harvested. Cut future stems at the base of the stem being harvested at the branching point. For the longest-lasting cut flowers, harvest when 1/3 of the tiny flowers that make up the flat bloom are open.

In the Landscape: Removing blooms as they fade, just above a leaf, will encourage fresh blooms and control self-seeding. To reinvigorate the growth of the plant, make an occasional cut deeper into the plant, as if harvesting for cut flowers.

FAVORITE VARIETIES:

For the garden and cutting: *Ammi majus*: 'Graceland', 'White Dill', 'Queen of Africa'; *Ammi visnaga*: 'Green Mist', all 36"- 48"

Bachelor Buttons § *Centaurea cyanus*

Bachelor buttons, sometimes called cornflowers, are one of the very earliest flowers to bloom in our garden. While the 'Blue Boy' is the most widely recognized for its intense blue color, there are other varieties that are just as noteworthy. Beneficial insects, like ladybugs and ground beetles, are attracted to this plant even when it is not blooming because the foliage also releases nectar – reason enough to grow this early spring plant!

FACTS TO GROW ON:

Full sun: 6-8 hours
Start from seed: Sow outdoors, do cover; sprouting in 7-14 days
Zone: Winter hardy to zone 6
Height: 24" - 36"
Spacing: Landscape 12"; Cutting 9"
Deer resistance: Excellent
Reseeding potential: Excellent
Container use: Good

TIPS TO FOR EASY SUCCESS:

Using flower support netting will easily keep the stems upright in the garden during wind and rainstorms.

WINTER STRATEGY:

Because of the strong winter hardiness trait of bachelor buttons, I would suggest gardeners one zone north of their winter hardiness zone try a fall planting. Covering with a single layer of floating row cover provides added protection. In zones 6 and south, no winter protection is needed.

KEEP THE BLOOMS COMING:

Blooms will continue into the hot summer if the faded flowers are removed on a regular basis.

For Cut Flowers: Make the first cut of the central stem at almost ground level, just above the lowest two to three leaves. Side shoots will develop and branch after the central stem is harvested. Cut future stems at the base of the stem being harvested. For the longest-lasting cut flowers, harvest when the bloom is just beginning to crack open and show color.

In the Landscape: Removal of the central stem of this plant will set it up to produce more stems and blooms over the long haul. Removal will also help to control the height of the plant, which is often the reason it tumbles over in the garden. To remove blooms as they fade, pinch just above a leaf. This will keep the garden full of fresh new flowers and can also control self-seeding.

FAVORITE VARIETIES:

For the garden, cutting, and containers: 'Boy Series', 'Formula Mix', 'Blue Boy', 'Pinkie', 'Black', 'Snowman', all 24" - 36"

Bells of Ireland § *Moluccella laevis*

Bells of Ireland are one of the most captivating flowers we grow. Visitors to our farm are intrigued, perplexed, and then wooed by this upright, branching green flower with bells running up the stem. Many have struggled to grow them in their own gardens, but the simple steps below will open the gate to success with this charming flower.

FACTS TO GROW ON:

Full sun: 6-8 hours
Start from seed: Sow outdoors, do not cover; sprouting 14-21 days
Zone: Winter hardy to zone 7
Height: 24" - 36"
Spacing: Landscape 12"; Cutting garden 9"
Deer resistance: Excellent
Reseeding potential: Good
Container use: Excellent

TIPS FOR EASY SUCCESS:

Rain can fill the bells with water, making them top heavy and causing them to tumble. Flower support netting is beneficial to keep these blooms upright in the garden.

SPECIAL SEED STARTING TIPS:

Place the seed packet in the freezer for 2 weeks prior to planting. Once removed from the freezer, soak the seeds for up to 5 days in water before planting. Pay close attention to the seedbed to keep it moist. This is a seed we always sow more generously than others to ensure a nice stand of plants.

WINTER STRATEGY:

Covering with a single or double layer of floating row cover helps to stabilize the environment in gardens like ours that have wide weather swings during winter.

KEEP THE BLOOMS COMING:

For Cut Flowers: Bells have a wide window of opportunity to harvest as a cut flower. Begin harvesting as soon as they reach a usable height. Make the cut at almost ground level, just above the lowest two side shoots. Side shoots will continue to mature into more substantial stems after the central stem is harvested. This plant grows taller with time and can be harvested as a fresh cut flower until it starts to turn beige. Once turning beige, they can be harvested to air dry for dried flowers.

In the Landscape: Bells tend not to grow new stems after cutting in regions with dry, hot, and humid summers, so in those areas deadheading is not necessary.

Slugs love bells of Ireland as much as we do. To rid your garden of these over-productive and destructive slimeballs, give them a saucer of beer to indulge in. The yeast in the beer is what draws them in and then, whoops...they fall in and drown!

Black-Eyed Susan § *Rudbeckia hirta*

Rudbeckia is a family of flowers that many recognize. But there are many more to grow than just those we see naturalized in fields. These plants are some of the best workhorses on our farm for producing large, beautiful, and long-lasting blooms. The fresh blooms and seed heads that develop are favorites of pollinators and songbirds.

FACTS TO GROW ON:

Part to full sun: 4-8 hours
Start from seed: Sow indoors, do not cover; or sow outdoors, do not cover; sprouting in 7-14 days
Zone: Winter hardy to zone 5
Height: 24" - 48"
Spacing: Landscape 12"; Cutting 9"
Deer resistance: Excellent
Reseeding potential: Excellent
Container use: Excellent

TIPS TO FOR EASY SUCCESS:

Leaving a few flower heads on the plants in the garden after they have faded will allow them to produce seed for songbirds and to naturally scatter in your garden. Recommended varieties are polite self-sowers. Using flower support netting will easily keep the taller varieties upright in the garden during wind and rainstorms.

WINTER STRATEGIES:

Black-eyed Susans are an easy target for slug damage because their young, tender leaves lie flat on the ground. For natural ways to rid your garden of these pests, see bottom note on page 50.

KEEP THE BLOOMS COMING:

For Cut Flowers: *Rudbeckia* stems grow from a cluster at the base of the plant. To encourage more stems to develop, make all the harvest cuts at the base, two to three inches above ground level. For the brightest and freshest cut flowers, harvest just after the petals have unfolded.

In the Landscape: Remove faded blooms just above a leaf. This will keep the garden producing fresh new flowers and can also control self-seeding. To reinvigorate the growth of the plant and to encourage more blooms, make an occasional cut deeper into the plant, as if harvesting for cut flowers.

FAVORITE VARIETIES:

For the garden and cutting: 'Indian Summer' 36"- 48", 'Double Daisy' 36", 'Prairie Sun' 24"- 30", 'Goldilocks' 24"- 30"

For containers: 'Prairie Sun' 24" - 30", 'Goldilocks' 24"- 30"

Bupleurum § *Bupleurum griffithii*

Bupleurum, commonly called hare's ear, is a wonderful garden plant and indispensable in fresh garden bouquets. Its flower head is a cluster of tiny yellow flowers that are beautiful in all stages, from fresh until it develops into a seed head. The foliage of bupleurum is as interesting as the flower; it appears as though the stem grows right through the leaf. This creates little crevises that hold drops of water after a rain shower, providing the much-needed moisture for the beneficial insects buzzing around these favored plants.

FACTS TO GROW ON:
Full sun: 6-8 hours
Start from seed: Sow outdoors, do cover; sprouting in 10-14 days
Zone: Winter hardy to zone 5
Height: 24"- 36"
Spacing: Landscape 12"; Cutting 9"
Deer resistance: Good
Reseeding potential: Excellent
Container use: Good

TIPS TO FOR EASY SUCCESS:
Leaving a few flower heads on the plants in the garden after they have faded will allow them to produce seed that will naturally scatter in your garden. Using flower support netting will easily keep the stems upright in the garden during wind and rainstorms.

SPECIAL SEED STARTING TIP:
Place seeds in the freezer for two weeks prior to planting.

WINTER STRATEGY:
Bupleurum is a tough winter survivor that makes it a very easy keeper. Regions that experience ample winter snow will learn that these seedlings thrive under snow cover.

KEEP THE BLOOMS COMING:
Cut Flowers: Make the first cut of the central stem at almost ground level, just above the lowest two to three side shoots. Side shoots will continue to grow, but new side shoot regrowth is limited. Harvest anytime, from when the tiny yellow flowers have begun to open until it develops its beautiful seed head. Harvesting too early in the bloom cycle will result in wilting.

Landscape: Because of the limited re-growth, leaving the blooms in the garden as long as possible extends the display. These flowers are beautiful for several weeks, but the heads should be removed before developing seeds to control self-seeding. The seed heads are a lovely addition to dried arrangements.

FAVORITE VARIETIES:
For the garden, cutting, and containers:
'Green Gold' 24"- 36"

Canterbury Bells § *Campanula medium*

Canterbury bells produces some of the most impressive heads of flowers on our farm. Also known as bellflower, it is a popular cottage garden flower that is a prolific producer of stems loaded with bells. While there are many varieties of *Campanula* to choose from, we have the greatest success with the annual variety 'Champion'. It blooms alongside some of the queens of spring in our garden: larkspur, digitalis and delphiniums, and is a real favorite of hummingbirds, bees and other pollinators. The bells that make up these voluminous flower heads hold water drops that provide the needed moisture to many beneficial insects.

FACTS TO GROW ON:

Full sun: 6-8 hours
Start from seed: Sow indoors, do not cover;
   sprouting in 14-21 days
Zone: Winter hardy to zone 5
Height: 24" - 30"
Spacing: Landscape 12"; Cutting 9"
Deer resistance: Poor
Reseeding potential: Slight
Container use: Excellent

TIPS TO FOR EASY SUCCESS:

When deer pressure is strong, plant in containers in a more protected area of the garden. Using flower support netting will keep these tall and heavy heads upright in the garden during wind and rainstorms.

WINTER STRATEGIES

Covering with a single layer of floating row cover will provide protection from deer damage through the winter before setting blooms. Routine spraying with deer repellent before blooming begins and throughout the season can prevent heavy damage.

KEEP THE BLOOMS COMING:

Canterbury bells will become a prolific producer of flowers in the garden if the faded flowers are removed on a regular basis.

For cut flowers: Stems tend to grow from a cluster at the base of the plant. To encourage more stems to develop, make all the harvest cuts at the base, one to two inches above ground level. More shoots will continue to develop and mature. Cut future stems at the base of the stem being harvested. For the freshest and longest-lasting cut flowers, harvest when the first 2-4 bells are open.

In the landscape: Remove heads of faded flowers just above a leaf. To reinvigorate the growth of the plant, make an occasional cut deeper into the plant, as if harvesting for cut flowers. This will keep this plant producing fresh new stems well in summer.

FAVORITE VARIETIES:

For the garden and cutting and containers:
'Champion Series' 24"- 30"

Corn Cockle § *Agrostemma githago*

One of the first bloomers in spring, corn cockle brings a pop of much-needed color early in the season. The 1-2" blooms grow in a spray (many branches on the stem with blooms) on a willowy stem. I love watching a group of these plants in bloom moving with the spring breezes – very relaxing! Although these blooms appear delicate, they hold up very well as a cut flower. Be sure to deadhead or harvest for cuts to extend their season. Otherwise, they tend to be just a flash of blooms in spring!

FACTS TO GROW ON:

Full sun: 6-8 hours
Start from seed: Sow outdoors, do cover; sprouting in 10-20 days
Zone: Winter hardy to zone 7
Height: 24"- 36"
Spacing: Landscape 8"; Cutting 6"
Deer resistance: Excellent
Reseeding potential: Good
Container use: Poor

TIPS TO FOR EASY SUCCESS:

We find that flower support netting is beneficial to keep these blooms upright in the garden. To prolong the life of corn cockle in warmer regions, plant them in a location that offers mid-to-late-afternoon shade.

WINTER STRATEGY TIPS:

Because of the strong winter hardiness trait of this plant, I would suggest gardeners one zone north of their winter hardiness zone try a fall planting. Cover with a lightweight floating row cover to stabilize the environment and give the plants the edge they need to survive colder temperatures.

KEEP THE BLOOMS COMING:

For Cut Flowers: This plant can be a challenge to harvest because its long, thin stems get tangled. To simplify, make the harvest cut at ground level, cutting the entire plant, knowing it will not regrow. As you hold the bottom of the stem, pull it down (out of the netting) instead of up (through the netting). Then, many stems can be cut from that entire plant. Selecting those plants with the most mature blooms will keep the patch fresh and continuing to bloom. For the freshest and longest-lasting cut flowers, harvest when the bud begins to crack open.

In the Landscape: Remove the blooms as they fade, just above a leaf. This will keep the garden full of fresh flowers and can also control self-seeding.

FAVORITE VARIETIES:

For the garden and cutting: 'Contessa Pale Pink' 36", 'Ocean Pearl' 24"- 30", 'Purple Queen' 24"- 30"

Delphinium § *Delphinium*

These absolutely beautiful spikes in shades of blue will become the highlight of your garden. They are nothing short of spectacular in a bouquet. Delphiniums are one of those perennials that can be grown as a hardy annual where conditions are warranted. Since hot and humid summers make it almost impossible for Delphiniums to survive, you can treat the flower as a fall-planted hardy annual – the perfect fix for such conditions.

FACTS TO GROW ON:

Full sun: 6-8 hours
Start from seed: Sow indoors, do cover; sprouting in 14-28 days
Zone: Winter hardy to zone 3
Height: 36" - 48"
Spacing: Landscape 12"; Cutting 12"
Deer resistance: Good
Reseeding potential: Slight
Container use: Poor

TIPS FOR EASY SUCCESS:

Plant transplants in the fall for the earliest and longest bloom period. You can forgo seed starting and order plants online. Delphiniums are widely available since they are also a commonly planted perennial. We find that flower support netting is essential to keep these blooms upright in the garden. To prolong blooming into summer, plant them in a location that offers mid-to-late-afternoon shade.

SPECIAL SEED STARTING TIPS:

Place seed packet in freezer for 2 weeks, remove and place seeds between moistened paper towels for 36 hours, then plant.

WINTER STRATEGIES:

Delphiniums are hardy to zone 3, so no winter protection is required.

KEEP THE BLOOMS COMING:

Cut Flowers: Make the *first cut* of the central stem, two to three inches above ground level. More shoots will continue to mature and develop after the central stem is harvested. Cut all future stems the same. For long-lasting cut flowers, harvest when the bottom 1/3 of the flowers on a stem are open.

Landscape: Remove blooms as they fade just, above a leaf. To reinvigorate the growth of the plant, make an occasional cut deeper into the plant, as if harvesting for cut flowers. This will keep the garden full of fresh new flowers.

FAVORITE VARIETIES:

For the garden and cutting: 'Pacific Giants' 36"- 48" and 'Oriental Series' 36".

Dill § *Anethum graveolens*

I can't imagine our garden without dill. The spectacular umbel blooms appear as fireworks bursting throughout the garden and it does the same in bouquets. The many tiny blooms that make up the large flower are very attractive to bees, butterflies, and other pollinators – all welcome guests.

FACTS TO GROW ON:

Full sun: 6-8 hours
Start from seed: Sow outdoors, do cover; or sow indoors, do cover; sprouting in 7-14 days
Zone: Winter hardy to zone 8
Height: 24"- 60"
Spacing: Landscape 8"; Cutting 6"
Deer resistance: Excellent
Reseeding potential: Excellent
Container use: Excellent

TIPS TO FOR EASY SUCCESS:

While fall or early spring plantings will offer the most robust plants, planting dill many times throughout the season will extend its benefits. As the summer heats up, plant in areas with afternoon shade. Leaving a few flower heads on the plants in the garden after they have faded will allow them to produce seed that will naturally scatter in your garden. Using flower support netting will easily keep the taller varieties upright in the garden during wind and rainstorms.

WINTER STRATEGIES:

Because of the strong winter hardiness trait of dill, I would suggest gardeners one zone north of the noted winter hardiness zone try a fall planting. Cover with a single or double layer of lightweight floating row cover to stabilize the environment and give dill the edge they need to survive colder temperatures. We do this here in zone 7 with great results.

KEEP THE BLOOMS COMING:

For Cut Flowers: Make the first cut of the central stem just above the lowest three to four side shoots. Cut future stems at the base of the stem. Dill has several stages of harvest. For fresh, bright yellow flowers, harvest when half of the tiny blooms are open. Skip cutting while the plant is making pollen and wait until it develops seeds to resume harvesting.

In the Landscape: Remove blooms as they fade, just above a leaf. This will encourage new blooms and can also control self-seeding. Harvest seeds to eat and replant.

FAVORITE VARIETIES:

For the garden and cutting: 'Bouquet' 36"- 60", 'Long Island Mammoth' 24"- 48"
For containers: 'Fernleaf' 24"- 32"

Dropmore § *Anchusa azurea*

Dropmore's large flower head and intensely blue blooms make it a standout feature in the early summer garden. A member of the same family as the well-known forget-me-not, but sporting larger, showier blooms, dropmore is one of those short-lived perennials that we grow as a hardy annual with excellent results.* As an edible flower, dropmore is beautiful in ice cubes and sprinkled on a salad. Bees and butterflies are especially attracted to this flower.

FACTS TO GROW ON:
Full sun: 6-8 hours
Start from seed: Sow indoors, do not cover; or sow outdoors, do not cover; sprouting in 14-28 days
Zone: Winter hardy to zone 3
Height: 36" – 48"
Spacing: Landscape 18"; Cutting 12"
Deer resistance: Good
Reseeding potential: Good
Container use: Good

TIPS TO FOR EASY SUCCESS:
Dropmore requires excellent drainage to prevent crown rot. These tall plants have large flower heads and will benefit from flower support netting to prevent tumbling during rainstorms. Leaving a few flower heads on the plants in the garden after they have faded will allow them to produce seed to naturally scatter in your garden. The plant will typically die and disappear in hot and humid summers.

KEEP THE BLOOMS COMING:
For Cut Flowers: Make the first cut of the central stem at almost ground level, just above the lowest two to three side shoots. Side shoots will continue to mature and develop branching after the central stem is harvested. Cut future stems at the base of the stem being harvested, at the branching point. For the longest-lasting cut flowers, harvest when ¼ of the individual flowers that make up the large flower head open. Harvest in early morning to prevent wilting.

In the Landscape: Removing blooms as they fade, just above a leaf, will encourage fresh blooms and control self-seeding. To reinvigorate the growth of the plant, make an occasional cut deeper into the plant as if harvesting for cut flowers.

*Other common names for dropmore are bugloss, italian bugloss and blue bugloss

False Queen Anne's Lace § *Daucus carota* var. *sativus*

This flower has become the "little black dress" of our garden – we love it because it is so useful! It is a member of the carrot family, but is grown for its very long lasting beautiful blooms. The bloom starts out as a mauve color which changes gradually to green! It is an asset in the garden and indispensable in the fresh bouquet. Bees and other pollinators flock to it.

FACTS TO GROW ON:

Full sun: 6-8 hours
Start from seed: Sow indoors, do cover; or sow outdoors, do cover; sprouting in 7-14 days
Zone: Winter hardy to zone 7
Height: 36"- 48"
Spacing: Landscape 12"; Cutting 9"
Deer resistance: Excellent
Reseeding potential: Excellent
Container use: Poor

TIPS FOR EASY SUCCESS:

We find that flower support netting is beneficial to keep these blooms upright in the garden. Leaving a few flower heads on the plants in the garden after they have faded will allow them to produce seed that will naturally scatter in your garden.

WINTER STRATEGIES:

Because of the strong winter hardiness trait of this plant, I would suggest gardeners one zone north of their winter hardiness zone try a fall planting. Cover with a lightweight floating row cover that will stabilize the environment and give the edge they need to survive colder temperatures. In our zone 7 garden this plant takes cold and wind with no problems, I suspect it would do quite well in zone 6.

KEEP THE BLOOMS COMING:

For Cut Flowers: Blooms may be harvested from the immature stage up through setting seed. Make the *first cut* of the central stem at almost ground level, just above the lowest two to three side shoots. Side shoots will continue to mature and branch after the central stem is harvested. Cut future stems at the base of the stem.

In the Landscape: Remove blooms as they fade, just above a branch. This will keep the garden full of fresh new flowers and can also control self-seeding. To reinvigorate the growth of the plant, make an occasional cut deeper into the plant, as if harvesting for cut flowers.

FAVORITE VARIETIES:

For the garden and cutting: 'Black Knight' 36" - 48"

Feverfew § *Tanacetum parthenium*

Frequently a part of the herb and cottage gardens, feverfew has earned a place of honor in our gardens for its delightful little button-like blooms. It makes an excellent cut flower, practically making a bouquet by itself. Its carefree nature makes it a really easy keeper in the garden. Feverfew repels all insects, including beneficials – so do not plant near plants that require pollination.

FACTS TO GROW ON:
Full sun: 6-8 hours
Start from seed: Sow indoors, do not cover; or sow outdoors, do not cover; sprouting in 7-14 days
Zone: Winter hardy to zone 5
Height: 30"- 48"
Spacing: Landscape 12"; Cutting 9"
Deer resistance: Excellent
Reseeding potential: Excellent
Container use: Good

TIPS FOR EASY SUCCESS:
Using flower support netting will easily keep the taller varieties upright in the garden during wind and rainstorms. Leaving a few flower heads on the plants in the garden after they have faded will allow them to produce seed that will naturally scatter in your garden.

WINTER STRATEGIES:
Because of the strong winter hardiness trait of feverfew, I would suggest gardeners one zone north of their winter hardiness zone try a fall planting. Cover with a lightweight floating row cover that will stabilize the environment and give the edge they need to survive colder temperatures. In regions with a winter snow cover, no row cover would be necessary.

KEEP THE BLOOMS COMING:
For Cut Flowers: Make the first cut of the central stem at almost ground level, just above the lowest three to four side shoots. Side shoots will continue to mature and develop branching after the central stem is harvested. Cut future stems at the base of the stem. For longest window of harvest begin cutting as soon as attractive through fully open.

In the Landscape: Remove fading blooms just above a leaf. This will keep the garden full of fresh new flowers and can also control self-seeding. To reinvigorate the growth of the plant, make an occasional cut deeper into the plant as if harvesting for cut flowers.

FAVORITE VARIETIES:
For the garden and cutting: 'Tetra White' 30"- 40", 'Virgo' 36", 'Feverfew' 36"- 48"

Foxglove § *Digitalis purpurea*

Foxgloves give a long-lasting show in the landscape, naturalized woodland setting, and cutting garden. We love growing "Foxy" because it has a great mix of colors with freckles and it is an annual that blooms the first year from seed. Hummingbirds, bees and other pollinators are especially fond of the tubular blossoms.

FACTS TO GROW ON:

Part to full sun: 4-8 hours
Start from seed: Sow indoors, do not cover; or sow outdoors, do not cover; sprouting in 7-14 days
Zone: Winter hardy to zone 5
Height: 24" - 36"
Spacing: Landscape 12"; Cutting 9"
Deer resistance: Excellent
Reseeding potential: Good
Container use: Excellent

TIPS FOR EASY SUCCESS:

Leaving a few flower heads on the plants in the garden after they have faded will allow them to produce seed that will naturally scatter in your garden. We find that flower support netting is beneficial to keep these blooms upright in the garden.

WINTER STRATEGIES:

A very winter-hardy plant, foxglove needs no attention during cold weather.

KEEP THE BLOOMS COMING:

Foxglove is a very prolific bloomer if it is planted in a location that offers mid-to-late-afternoon shade and faded blooms are removed on a regular basis.

For Cut Flowers: Make the harvest cut at the base of the stem at ground level; more shoots will continue to grow from the base and develop into nice stems. For the longest-lasting cut flowers, harvest when the first flower on the bottom of the stem opens.

In the Landscape: Remove the blooms as they fade, just above a leaf. This will keep the garden full of new flowers and can also control self-seeding. To reinvigorate the growth of the plant, make an occasional cut deeper into the plant as if harvesting for cut flowers.

FAVORITE VARIETIES:

For the garden, cutting and containers: 'Foxy' 24"- 36"

Note: All parts of foxgloves are considered poisonous.

Godetia § *Clarkia amoena*

This beautiful flower is sometimes called "farewell to spring" because it blooms just as spring is fading into summer. It is an outstanding cut flower and once you've tried it in your garden, you won't want to do without. Butterflies and pollinators are especially fond of the clusters of satiny blooms at the top of each stem.

FACTS TO GROW ON:

Full sun: 6-8 hours

Start from seed: Sow indoors, do not cover; or sow outdoors, do not cover; sprouting in 14-21 days

Zone: Winter hardy to zone 8

Height: 20"- 30"

Spacing: Landscape 12"; Cutting 9"

Deer resistance: Good

Reseeding potential: Excellent

Container use: Excellent

TIPS FOR EASY SUCCESS:

We find that flower support netting is beneficial to keep blooms upright in the garden. To prolong blooming, plant in a location that offers mid-to-late-afternoon shade. Leaving a few flower heads on the plants in the garden after they have faded will allow them to produce seed that will naturally scatter in your garden.

SPECIAL SEED STARTING TIP:

Godetia needs temperatures on the cooler side to germinate.

WINTER STRATEGIES:

We plant transplants out in the garden up to 10 weeks before our last frost date, with a floating row cover for protection. This plant thrives under cold conditions – it just can't survive prolonged freezing temperatures.

KEEP THE BLOOMS COMING:

For Cut Flowers: Make the first cut of the central stem at almost ground level, just above the lowest two to three side shoots. Side shoots will continue to mature and branch after the central stem is harvested. Cut future stems at the base of the stem being harvested, at the branching point. For the freshest and longest-lasting cut flowers, harvest just as the bloom begins to open.

In the Landscape: Remove blooms as they fade, just above a leaf. To encourage self-seeding, leave as many flowers as possible in the garden to develop seeds. If summer heats up quickly, there will not be much regrowth.

FAVORITE VARIETIES:

For the garden, cutting and containers: 'Flamingo Series' 20"- 30", 'Grace Series' 20"- 24"

Ornamental Kale § *Brassica oleracea*

From garnishing the Thanksgiving table to fall bouquets and containers, kale is versatile and beautiful. Their ability to continue the show in spring makes them a perfect companion to pansies. Growing the longer stemmed varieties for cut flowers is a newer novelty and beautiful in fall and winter bouquets. A bonus: their colors intensify as the temperatures drop.

FACTS TO GROW ON:

Full sun: 6-8 hours
Start from seed: Sow indoors, do cover; sprouting in 10-14 days
Zone: Winter hardy to zone 7
Height: 10"- 30"
Spacing: Landscape 12"; Cutting 3"- 6"
Deer resistance: Excellent
Reseeding potential: Poor
Container use: Excellent

TIPS FOR EASY SUCCESS:

For the taller cut-flower varieties, use flower support netting to keep the heavy heads upright in the garden during wind and rainstorms.

WINTER STRATEGIES:

Because of the strong winter hardiness trait of this plant, I would suggest gardeners one zone north of their winter hardiness zone try a fall planting. Cover with pine straw or a lightweight floating row cover to stabilize the environment and give the plants the edge they need to survive colder temperatures.

KEEP THE BLOOMS COMING:

For Cut Flowers: Cut-flower kale typically has only one stem. On occasion, after the central stem has been harvested, it may develop side shoots that can grow and become a useable stem. Stems can be cut at any point during development. Strip the leaves along the stem leaving only the top 3-4". The leaves make an excellent garnish.

In the Landscape: To keep kale looking its best, both in containers and the garden, you can provide protection when dry, cold temperatures are expected. Containers can be brought into a garage. Out in the garden, you can protect the beautiful leaves by placing a layer of pine straw in the landscape over the plants.

FAVORITE VARIETIES:

For the garden and containers: 'White Peacock' 12"- 18", 'Nagoya Hybrid Mixed' 8"
For cutting: 'Crane Mix' 24"- 36"

The same cabbage loopers that eat broccoli can be a problem for ornamental kales. The white moths you see flying around the garden are the troublemakers laying the eggs that develop into the caterpillars that eat holes in the plants. Treat with BT (Bacillus thuringensis), an organic product that eliminates the caterpillars without causing harm to beneficial insects or wildlife. Begin treating in late summer to prevent a population explosion.

Lambada § *Monarda hybrida*

This flower should appear in gardens more often. Lambada, a member of the well-known bee balm family, has beautiful pink-lavender blooms that are even more gorgeous right before they bloom, in the silvery-green stage. It is very easy to start from seed and less likely to encounter powdery mildew than others in this family. Lambada thrives through hot and dry conditions. Bees and hummingbirds adore these blooms.

FACTS TO GROW ON:

Full sun: 6-8 hours
Start from seed: Sow indoors, do cover; or sow outdoors, do cover; sprouting in 7-14 days
Zone: Winter hardy to zone 7
Height: 24"- 36"
Spacing: Landscape 12"; Cutting 9"
Deer resistance: Excellent
Reseeding potential: Good
Container use: Good

TIPS FOR EASY SUCCESS:

We find that flower support netting is beneficial to keep these blooms upright in the garden. Leaving a few flower heads on the plants in the garden after they have faded will allow them to produce seed that will naturally scatter.

WINTER STRATEGIES:

Because of the strong winter hardiness trait of this plant, I would suggest gardeners one zone north of their winter hardiness zone try a fall planting. Cover with a lightweight floating row cover that will stabilize the environment and give the edge they need to survive colder temperatures.

KEEP THE BLOOMS COMING:

For Cut Flowers: Make the first cut of the central stem at almost ground level, just above the lowest two to three side shoots. Side shoots will continue to mature and branch after the central stem is harvested. Cut future stems at the base of the stem being harvested, at the branching point. For long-lasting cut flowers, harvest once the blooms begin to turn pink. If wilting is a problem, try removing excessive foliage.

In the Landscape: Remove blooms as they fade, just above a leaf or branch. This will keep the garden full of fresh new flowers and can also control self-seeding. To reinvigorate the growth of the plant, make an occasional cut deeper into the plant, as if harvesting for cut flowers.

Larkspur § *Delphinium consolida*

The beautiful stately spikes of larkspur can stand over 4 feet tall. Easily grown from seed, Larkspur can be planted all one color or as a mix of colors. They are beautiful either way! Scattered among spring blooming perennials, larkspur is a polite and perfect companion in the mixed border. Hummingbirds, bees, and other pollinators are frequent visitors to the larkspur patch.

FACTS TO GROW ON:

Full sun: 6-8 hours
Start from seed: Sow outdoors, do cover; sprouting in 14-28 days
Zone: Winter hardy to zone 6
Height: 36"- 48"
Spacing: Landscape 9"; Cutting 6"
Deer resistance: Good
Reseeding potential: Excellent
Container use: Poor

TIPS FOR EASY SUCCESS:

We find that flower support netting is beneficial to keep these blooms upright in the garden. Leaving a few flower heads on the plants after they have faded will allow them to produce seed that will naturally scatter in your garden.

WINTER STRATEGIES:

Covering with a lightweight floating row cover for winter will stabilize the environment and help to produce a more robust plant that may bloom a bit earlier.

KEEP THE BLOOMS COMING:

For Cut Flowers: Make the harvest cut at the base of the stem at ground level. More shoots will continue to develop from the base and grow into nice stems. For the freshest and longest lasting cut flowers, harvest when the first flower on the bottom of the stem is open.

In the Landscape: Remove blooms as they fade, just above a leaf. This will keep fresh flowers coming for as long as possible and can control self-seeding.

FAVORITE VARIETIES:

For the garden and cutting: 'Sublime', 'QIS Series', and 'Giant Imperial', all 36"-48"

Larkspur blooming in a peony patch makes for a grand show in spring. To encourage self-seeding, leave some of the flower heads in the garden to produce seed to scatter naturally. Mulch should be no more than one or two inches deep so the seeds can make contact with soil. Be sure to scout for self-sown seedlings the following season.

Lisianthus § *Eustoma*

Because of its needy reputation, I avoided growing lisianthus for years. Once I finally tried, I discovered it wasn't difficult at all. When given the conditions it loves, lisianthus becomes a thriving member of the garden. Gorgeous rose-like blooms make this plant a fabulous addition to any garden or bouquet. The delicate but long-lasting blooms thrive in midsummer's heat.

FACTS TO GROW ON:

Full sun: 6-8 hours
Start from seed: Sow indoors, do not cover; sprouting in 10-14 days (see note, below)
Zone: Winter hardy to zone 7
Height: 12"- 36"
Spacing: Landscape 6"; Cutting 4"- 6"
Deer resistance: Excellent
Reseeding potential: Poor
Container use: Excellent

Seed Starting Note:

Start seed 12-16 weeks before transplanting seedlings to the garden, in conditions below 75 degrees.

TIPS FOR EASY SUCCESS:

Excellent drainage and a little afternoon shade are the secrets to success with lisianthus. Growing in large containers is a great choice for areas that have poor drainage. We find that flower support netting is beneficial to keep these blooms upright in the garden.

WINTER STRATEGIES:

Because of the strong winter hardiness trait of lisianthus, I would suggest gardeners one zone north of their winter hardiness zone try a fall planting. Cover with a lightweight floating row cover that will stabilize the environment and give the plants the edge they need to survive colder temperatures.

KEEP THE BLOOMS COMING:

For Cut Flowers: Make the first cut of the central stem at almost ground level, just above the lowest two to three side shoots. Side shoots will continue to mature and branch after the central stem is harvested. Cut future stems at the base of the stem being harvested, at the branching point. For longest-lasting cut flowers, harvest when 3-4 flowers are open. Expect a second flush of blooms 1-2 months after the initial blooms.

In the Landscape: Remove blooms as they fade, just above a leaf. This will keep the garden full of fresh flowers. To reinvigorate the growth of the plant for the second flush of blooms, remove the stems, making deeper cuts into the plant as if harvesting for cut flowers.

FAVORITE VARIETIES:

For the garden and cutting: 'Mariachi' 20"- 30", 'ABC Series' 24"- 36", 'Echo' 24"- 30".
For containers: 'Mariachi' 20"- 30"

Love-in-a-Mist § *Nigella*

Love-in-a-mist is an old-fashioned flower commonly found in cottage gardens. The blooms are available in great hues of blue, rose, and even white. The pod that follows the bloom also varies in color. From the green pods of 'Albion Green Marbles' to the striped pod of 'Mrs. Jekyll', this flower is fabulous fresh or dried. The lacey, fernlike foliage is another great feature of this delightful little flower. While its strong ability to self-seed delights most, it can be troublesome to others. We appreciate all the volunteer plants and simply remove any unwanted seedlings with a hoe.

FACTS TO GROW ON:

Full sun: 6-8 hours
Start from seed: Sow outdoors, do cover;
  sprouting in 14-21 days
Zone: Winter hardy to zone 6
Height: 18"- 24"
Spacing: Landscape 9"; Cutting 6"
Deer resistance: Excellent
Reseeding potential: Excellent
Container use: Excellent

TIPS FOR EASY SUCCESS:

Grow different varieties to extend the bloom time. Leaving a few seed pods on the plants in the garden after they have developed will allow them to scatter naturally.

WINTER STRATEGIES:

Because of the strong winter hardiness trait of love-in-a mist, I would suggest gardeners one zone north of their winter hardiness zone try a fall planting. Cover with a lightweight floating row cover that will stabilize the environment and give the edge they need to survive colder temperatures.

KEEP THE BLOOMS COMING:

For Cut Flowers: Make the first cut of the central stem at almost ground level, just above the lowest three to four side shoots. Side shoots will continue to develop into usable stems to harvest. Cut future stems at the base of the stem being harvested at the branching point. *Nigella* can be harvested from the moment the blooms are cracking open until the seed pod has developed. For dried flowers, cut while the pod is fresh and still green. Hang to dry.

In the Landscape: Removing the faded blooms may encourage more flowers, but it also removes future pod development. To control self-seeding, remove all heads on the plants before the pods burst open.

FAVORITE VARIETIES:

For the garden, cutting and container:
N. damascene: 'Albion Series' 24", 'Persian Series' 18", 'Miss Jekyll' 20", 'Cramer's Plum' 18"- 24",
N. orientalis: 'Transformer' 24".

Pansy § *Viola* x *wittrockiana*

I have the fondest memories as a girl at Easter time, bringing home a pansy I planted in a little cup at Sunday school. These little smiling faces of spring have grown even more popular with the endless colors available and their carefree nature. Perhaps my all-time favorite container combos are pansies and tulips. The pansies are pretty for fall and winter and then in spring the tulips pop through the pansies for the grand appearance.

FACTS TO GROW ON:

Part to full sun: 4-8 hours
Start from seed: Sow indoors, do cover; sprouting in 14-21 days
Zone: Winter hardy to zone 7
Height: 8"- 12"
Spacing: Landscape 9"- 12"
Deer resistance: Poor
Reseeding potential: Good
Container use: Excellent

TIPS FOR EASY SUCCESS:
Assorted colors of potted pansies are widely available from your local garden centers at the correct planting time for your area.

SPECIAL SEED STARTING TIP:
Starting pansies from seed is easy – it just takes 10-12 weeks to grow a plant large enough to plant outdoors.

WINTER STRATEGIES:
Routine spraying with deer repellent before blooming begins and throughout the season can be successful in preventing heavy damage. Covering with a single layer of floating row cover will provide protection from dry winter wind and deer damage through the winter.

KEEP THE BLOOMS COMING:
For Cut Flowers: Although pansies are not known for their cut flowers, they do provide some of the sweetest little blooms during cold weather that are perfect for the kitchen table. Cut stems at their base in all stages of opening.

In the Landscape and Containers: Pinching the faded blooms weekly will have your pansies blooming non-stop. In the landscape, to encourage self-seeding, leave a few of the faded blooms to develop seeds.

FAVORITE VARIETIES:
For the garden and containers: 'Delta Series' 8", 'Bingo Series' 8".

Pincushion Flower § *Scabiosa Atropurpurea*

Pincushion flower is the favorite of bumblebees on our farm. Because of this, I always do necessary chores for this patch first thing in the morning before the bees are up. The button-like bud colors up before it begins to bloom, making pincushion flower a long-lasting contributor to the garden and in bouquets.

FACTS TO GROW ON:

Full sun: 6-8 hours
Start from seed: Sow indoors, do cover; or sow outdoors, do cover; sprouting in 14-21 days
Zone: Winter hardy to zone 7
Height: 24"-36"
Spacing: Landscape 12"; Cutting 9"
Deer resistance: Good
Reseeding potential: Good
Container use: Good

TIPS FOR EASY SUCCESS:

Using flower support netting will easily keep the taller varieties upright in the garden during wind and rainstorms.

WINTER STRATEGIES:

Covering with a single layer of floating row cover provides enough protection to result in a more robust plant than those left uncovered.

KEEP THE BLOOMS COMING:

When harvested for cuts or deadheaded regularly, the pincushion flower is a prolific bloomer.

For Cut Flowers: Make the first cut of the central stem at almost ground level, just above the lowest two to three side shoots. Side shoots will continue to mature and develop. Cut future stems at the base of the stem. For long-lasting cut flowers, harvest when the first ⅓ of tiny flowers are open.

In the Landscape: Remove blooms as they fade, just above a leaf. To reinvigorate the growth of the plant, make an occasional cut deeper into the plant, as if harvesting for cut flowers.

FAVORITE VARIETIES:

For the garden, cutting and containers: 'Fire King', 'Blue Cockade', 'Black Knight', all 24"- 36"

Want a more abundant tomato harvest? Try planting pincushion flowers as a companion to tomatoes in order to attract bumblebees. Why? Tomatoes are self-pollinating plants, meaning they have both the male and female parts necessary to produce fruit in each flower. The pollen falls from the male stamen onto the female stigma and the pollination eventually produces a tomato. When a bumblebee visits a tomato flower, its buzzing motion increases the action. This can result in more and larger tomatoes.

Iceland Poppy § *Papaver Nudicaule*

These delicate crepe-like blooms appear in spring – perfect along a walkway or in a container. When grown in mass, this poppy brings texture to the garden like no other. The Iceland poppy is easy to grow and, if it is happy with where you plant its seed, will return year after year by self-seeding. We grow the variety 'Champagne Bubbles' because it will last in a vase for a several days without special handling. It features a beautiful mix of colors: creamy-white, salmon-orange, yellow, coral-pink, and red. The wide-faced blossoms also attract bees and other pollinators.

FACTS TO GROW ON:

Full sun: 6-8 hours
Start from seed: Sow outdoors, do not cover;
  sprouting in 14-21 days
Zone: Winter hardy to zone 6
Height: 12"- 18"
Spacing: Landscape 9"; Cutting 6"
Deer resistance: Excellent
Reseeding potential: Excellent
Container use: Excellent

TIPS FOR EASY SUCCESS:

Birds really like poppy seeds, so cover your seed planting with a lightweight floating row cover until they have germinated. Leaving a few flower heads in the garden after the flowers have faded will allow them to produce seed that will naturally scatter.

WINTER STRATEGIES:

Iceland Poppies, as the name implies, are very winter hardy. Because of the strong winter hardiness trait of this plant, I would suggest gardeners one zone north of their winter hardiness zone try a fall planting. Cover with a lightweight floating row cover to stabilize the environment and give the plants the edge they need to survive even colder temperatures.

KEEP THE BLOOMS COMING:

For Cut Flowers: Poppy stems grow from a cluster at the base of the plant. Make the harvest cut at the base of the stem at ground level. More shoots will continue to develop and mature. For the freshest and longest-lasting cut flowers, harvest when the bud just begins to crack open and you can see the color of the bloom.

In the Landscape: When you remove the stems and heads of faded blooms you are encouraging more blooming – however, keep in mind that the amount of pods you leave in the garden dictates the degree of reseeding that will occur.

FAVORITE VARIETIES:

For the garden, cutting and containers: 'Champagne Bubbles' 12"- 18"

Pot Marigold *Calendula officinialis*

The pot marigold produces large, daisy-like double blooms that are most often seen in orange, but also come in creamy white and a beautiful yellow. We refer to them as our "spring zinnias" because of the shape of the bloom and the hot colors – not so common in other spring bloomers. Pot marigold is one of the first bloomers in spring for us, and provides a very long window of blooms when we keep the patch free from faded flowers.

FACTS TO GROW ON:

Part to full sun: 4-8 hours
Start from seed: Sow indoors, do cover; or sow outdoors, do cover; sprouting in 10-14 days
Zone: Winter hardy to zone 7
Height: 12"- 24"
Spacing: Landscape 9"; Cutting 6"
Deer resistance: Good
Reseeding potential: Good
Container use: Excellent

TIPS FOR EASY SUCCESS:

We find that flower support netting is beneficial to keep the taller blooms upright in the garden. To prolong blooming into a hot summer, plant pot marigolds in a location that offers mid-to-late-afternoon shade. Leaving a few flower heads on the plants after they have faded will allow them to produce seed that will naturally scatter in your garden.

WINTER STRATEGIES:

Covering with a single layer of floating row cover provides enough protection to produce a more robust plant and earlier blooms than those left uncovered.

KEEP THE BLOOMS COMING:

Pot marigolds are non-stop producers of blooms when harvested or deadheaded regularly.

For Cut Flowers: Harvest stems at ground level – I sometimes even cut a little into the ground for more length when needed. The more you harvest, the more nice stems it will give. For the freshest and longest-lasting cut flowers, harvest when the blooms just begin to crack open.

In the Landscape: Remove the stem of the faded flower at ground level. This will keep the garden full of fresh new flowers and can also control self-seeding.

FAVORITE VARIETIES:

For the garden, cutting and containers: 'Pacific Beauties Series' 24", 'Prince Series' 24", and 'Princess Series' 20"- 24".

Snapdragon § *Antirrhinum majus*

It was my success and pure delight with growing snapdragons that began my journey into hardy annual gardening. I look forward to their vigor and the sweet fragrance each year that announces spring has arrived on our farm. One of the most productive and long-lived spring flowers we grow, snaps are also a favorite of bees and hummingbirds.

FACTS TO GROW ON:

Full sun: 6-8 hours
Start from seed: Sow indoors, do not cover; sprouting in 3-7 days
Zone: Winter hardy to zone 4, varieties may vary
Height: 24" - 36"
Spacing: Landscape 12"; Cutting garden 9"
Deer resistance: Good
Reseeding potential: Slight
Container use: Excellent

Harvest Note:

A visit from a bee or hummingbird leads to premature death for blooms. So for longer-lasting cut flowers, harvest just as the first bottom flower opens to prevent pollination.

TIPS FOR EASY SUCCESS:

Snapdragons are one of the hardiest growers for fall planting and winter survival. The very earliest to bloom is 'Chantilly', coming in 4 weeks earlier than the others, followed by 'Opus', 'Madame Butterfly' and then 'Rocket'. Using flower support netting will easily keep the taller varieties upright in the garden during wind and rainstorms.

WINTER STRATEGIES:

Covering with a single layer of floating row cover provides enough protection to result in a more robust plant come spring and perhaps blooms earlier than plants left uncovered.

KEEP THE BLOOMS COMING:

Snapdragons will bloom into summer if the blooms are removed on a regular basis.

For Cut Flowers: Make the first cut of the central stem at almost ground level, just above the lowest two to three side shoots. Side shoots will continue to mature and branch after the central stem has been harvested. Cut future stems at the base of the stem at the branching point. Harvest when the first bottom flower opens.

In the Landscape: If you are going to forgo harvesting cut flowers, remove blooms as they fade, just above a leaf. To reinvigorate the growth of the plant, make an occasional cut deeper into the plant, as if harvesting for cut flowers. This will keep the garden full of fresh new flowers.

FAVORITE VARIETIES:

For the garden and cutting: 'Chantilly' 36", 'Opus' 36", 'Madame Butterfly' 30", 'Rocket' 36"

For containers: 'Sonnet', 24"

Strawflower § *Helichrysum bracteatum*

Strawflowers are one of the favorites on our farm – its colors are vibrant and beautiful, and the blooms last a really long time. Strawflowers are easy to preserve as a dry flower for winter bouquets, but its real calling is to be on display in fresh bouquets and in the garden. Butterflies, native bees and other pollinators are attracted to the florets in the center of the bloom.

FACTS TO GROW ON:

Full sun: 6-8 hours
Start from seed: Sow indoors, do not cover; or sow
   outdoors, do not cover; sprouting in 7-10 days
Zone: Winter hardy to zone 8
Height: 12"- 36"
Spacing: Landscape 12"; Cutting 9"
Deer resistance: Excellent
Reseeding potential: Slight
Container use: Excellent

TIPS FOR EASY SUCCESS:

Using flower support netting will easily keep the taller varieties upright in the garden during wind and rainstorms.

WINTER STRATEGIES:

We plant transplants out in the garden up to 10 weeks before our last frost date, with a floating row cover for protection. This plant thrives under cold conditions – it just can't survive prolonged freezing temperatures. An early start in cool conditions lends to a more robust plant.

KEEP THE BLOOMS COMING:

For Cut Flowers: Make the first cut of the central stem at almost ground level, just above the lowest three to four side shoots. Side shoots will continue to mature and branch after the central stem is harvested. Cut future stems at the base of the stem to encourage regrowth. For fresh flowers, harvest when the center is developed and the bracts, which look like petals, are almost completely unfolded. For dried use, allow the flower to fully open, harvest, and hang to air dry in a well-ventilated area.

In the Landscape: Strawflower blooms last a long time in the garden. Remove those that become unattractive just above a leaf. This will keep the garden full of fresh flowers.

FAVORITE VARIETIES:

For the garden and cutting: 'Bright Bikini Mix' 12", 'King Size Formula Mix' 24"- 36", 'Cut-Flower Series' 36"

Sweet Pea § *Lathyrus Odoratus*

Fragrant sweet pea blossoms are perhaps the most romantic flower ever grown. They have a power that causes their admirers to linger in the garden and even clip some sweet peas to carry inside. While the blossoms last only 5-7 days in a vase, I have been told by flower lovers that it is the best 5 days ever! It can be a struggle to grow these flowers for those living in regions with hot summers, because they are often planted too late. Depending on the region, sweet peas thrive best when planted in fall (as we do here in zone 7) or in very early spring in colder areas.

FACTS TO GROW ON:

Full sun: 6-8 hours
Start from seed: Sow indoors, do cover; or sow outdoors, do cover; sprouting in 7-10 days
Zone: Winter hardy to zone 7
Height: Vines 36"- 72", Stems 8"- 14"
Spacing: Landscape 12"; Cutting 12"
Deer resistance: Good
Reseeding potential: Slight
Container use: Excellent

TIPS FOR EASY SUCCESS:
Excellent drainage is a must for sweet peas. Use vertical support netting on strong posts or provide a decorative trellis that will keep the vines upright in the garden.

SPECIAL SEED STARTING TIP:
Before planting, soak seeds in lukewarm water for 1-3 hours, then plant immediately.

WINTER STRATEGIES:
Covering with a single or double layer of floating row cover will give added winter protection in colder regions and produce a more robust vine earlier in the season.

KEEP THE BLOOMS COMING:
Harvesting or deadheading sweet pea vines on a regular basis will keep new blooms developing well into summer.

For Cut Flowers: Make the cut at the base of the stem. Harvest sweet pea blooms when half to fully open; they do not continue to open after cutting. When taller stems are needed, cut the vine with several stems of blooms and use it as a stem. The vine will regrow in favorable growing conditions.

In the Landscape: Removing the faded flowers weekly will keep the vines producing. There are no benefits to leaving the stem of a faded flower – so make the cut at the base of the stem to remove. This will keep the garden full of fresh new flowers. To encourage reseeding, let some seed pods develop to self-seed.

FAVORITE VARIETIES:
For the garden and cutting: 'Spencer Series', 'High Scent', and 'Royal Mix'.
For containers: 'Knee-Hi Mix' 36" (vine)

Sweet William § *Dianthus barbatus*

This family of plants puts on a long-lasting show in the garden and in bouquets making sweet William a must-have for every spring garden. The delicate fragrance of sweet William is no indication of its rough and tough nature. It is one of the winter-hardiest plants we grow, taking the extreme weather swings we experience with no problem. The 'Sweet Series' is one of the first flowers to bloom in our garden, followed by 'Amazon', which does very well in the summer heat.

FACTS TO GROW ON:
Part to full sun: 4-8 hours
Start from seed: Sow indoors, do not cover;
  sprouting in 7-14 days
Zone: Winter hardy to zone 5
Height: 18"- 30"
Spacing: Landscape 12"; Cutting 9"
Deer resistance: Excellent
Reseeding potential: Slight
Container use: Excellent

TIPS FOR EASY SUCCESS:
Using flower support netting will easily keep the taller varieties upright in the garden during wind and rainstorms. To prolong blooming into a hot summer, plant them in a location that offers mid-to-late-afternoon shade.

WINTER STRATEGIES:
Covering with a single layer of floating row cover provides enough protection to result in a more robust plant that may bloom earlier than those left uncovered.

KEEP THE BLOOMS COMING:
For Cut Flowers: Make the first cut of the central stem at almost ground level, just above the lowest two to three side shoots. Side shoots will continue to mature and branch after the central stem is harvested. Cut future stems at the base of the stem being harvested. For long-lasting cut flowers, harvest when 1/3 of the flowers are open.

In the Landscape: If you are going to forgo harvesting cut flowers, then remove blooms as they fade, just above a leaf. This will keep the garden full of fresh new flowers. To reinvigorate the growth of the plant, make an occasional cut deeper into the plant, as if harvesting for cut flowers.

FAVORITE VARIETIES:
For the garden and cutting: 'Sweet Series' 18"- 24", 'Amazon Series' 24"- 30", and 'Newport Pink' 20".
For containers: 'Sweet' 18"- 24"and 'Newport Pink' 20"

Throatwort § *Trachelium caeruleum*

This pretty flower really got the short end of the stick when it came to naming. I prefer to call it by its botanical name, *Trachelium*, to give it the dignity it deserves! While not the brightest star in the garden, *Trachelium* is one of those background flowers that make all the others shine a bit more. Butterflies and other beneficial insects are attracted to all the tiny little blossoms that make up this large flat flower.

FACTS TO GROW ON:

Part to full sun: 4-8 hours
Start from seed: Sow indoors, do not cover; sprouting in 7-14 days
Zone: Winter hardy to zone 7
Height: 24"- 30"
Spacing: Landscape 12"; Cutting 9"
Deer resistance: Excellent
Reseeding potential: Good
Container use: Excellent

TIPS FOR EASY SUCCESS:

To prolong blooming into a hot summer, plant *Trachelium* in a location that offers mid-to-late-afternoon shade. Leaving a few flower heads on the plants in the garden after they have faded will allow them to produce seed that will naturally scatter in your garden.

WINTER STRATEGIES:

Covering with a single layer of floating row cover provides enough protection to result in more robust plants in spring than those left uncovered.

KEEP THE BLOOMS COMING:

For Cut Flowers: Stems grow from a cluster at ground level. Make the harvest cut at ground level and more shoots will continue to mature and develop. For long-lasting cut flowers, harvest when 1/3 of the tiny flowers have opened.

In the Landscape: Remove blooms as they fade, just above a leaf. To reinvigorate the growth of the plant, make an occasional cut deeper into the plant, as if harvesting for cut flowers. This will keep the garden full of fresh new flowers and can also control self-seeding.

FAVORITE VARIETIES:

For the garden, cutting and containers: 'Shine' and 'Lake Michigan Mix', both 24"- 36".

White Lace Flower § *Orlaya grandiflora*

When I grew this delightful plant the first time, I thought it would be similar to, *Ammi majus* – but I was wrong. The more compact growth habit of white lace makes it a great fit in the landscape. The delicate umbel lacey blooms are unique, with larger petals around the edges of the bloom. White lace is always a welcome addition to a fresh garden bouquet and a real favorite of bees, butterflies and other pollinators.

FACTS TO GROW ON:
Full sun: 6-8 hours
Start from seed: Sow indoors, do not cover; or sow outdoors, do not cover; sprouting in 14-21 days
Zone: Winter hardy to zone 6
Height: 24"
Spacing: Landscape 12"; Cutting 9"
Deer resistance: Good
Reseeding potential: Excellent
Container use: Excellent

TIPS TO FOR EASY SUCCESS
To prolong the life of white lace flowers into a hot summer, plant them in a location that offers mid-to-late-afternoon shade. Leaving a few flower heads on the plants in the garden after they have faded will allow them to produce seeds that will naturally scatter in your garden.

WINTER STRATEGIES
Covering with a single layer of floating row cover provides enough protection to result in blooms earlier than those left uncovered.

KEEP THE BLOOMS COMING
For Cut Flowers: To encourage this plant to produce more stems that are as tall as possible, make all the harvest cuts just above ground level. This will encourage more stems to develop from the base of the plant. For long-lasting cut flowers, harvest when the first ⅓ of flowers are open.

In the Landscape: This flower will produce more blooms, as long as you remove blooms as they fade, just above the leaf. This will keep the garden full of fresh new flowers and can also control self-seeding. To reinvigorate the growth of the plant, make an occasional cut deeper into the plant, as if harvesting for cut flowers.

Yarrow § *Achillea Millefolium*

The large, flat-topped blooms of yarrow come in an assortment of colors – including peach, lavender, red, pink and ivory – that make them a perfect addition to the garden and in bouquets. The yarrow family is quite large and has many members to choose from (some better behaved than others). The varieties that we grow tend to be short-lived perennials, which is why we grow them as a hardy annual. Some of the most beautiful colors can only be obtained by replanting annually. They are irresistible to butterflies and other pollinators, and provide excellent habitat for beneficial insects to raise babies.

FACTS TO GROW ON:

Full sun: 6-8 hours
Start from seed: Sow indoors, do not cover; or sow outdoors, do not cover; sprouting in 7-14 days
Zone: Winter hardy to zone 4
Height: 24"- 36"
Spacing: Landscape 9"- 12"; Cutting 9"
Deer resistance: Excellent
Reseeding potential: Excellent
Container use: Good

TIPS FOR EASY SUCCESS:

Using flower support netting will easily keep the taller varieties upright in the garden during wind and rainstorms.

WINTER STRATEGIES:

Yarrow is very winter hardy – no care or protection required.

KEEP THE BLOOMS COMING:

Yarrow will continue to produce new flowers as long as the faded flowers are removed weekly.

For Cut Flowers: Stems grow from a cluster at ground level. Make the harvest cut at ground level and more shoots will continue to mature and develop. For long-lasting cut flowers, harvest when at least $2/3$ of the tiny flowers have opened. Harvesting too early can result in the flower wilting. To dry, harvest when fully developed and hang to dry in a well-ventilated area.

In the Landscape: Remove blooms as they fade, just above a leaf. This will keep the garden full of new flowers and can also control self-seeding. To reinvigorate the growth of the plant, make an occasional cut deeper into the plant, as if harvesting for cut flowers.

FAVORITE VARIETIES:

For the garden, cutting and container: 'Colorado Sunset' and 'Summer Berries', both 24"- 36".

Just sprouted False Queen Anne's Lace.

Six

STARTING FROM SEED

At the root of a great garden, you will likely find a gardener who loves to start plants from seeds. Whether planting the seeds directly into garden soil or starting them indoors, seed starting opens a whole new world for the gardener. No other success in the garden brings such satisfaction.

Starting your own plants at the right time is the only way to be sure of having a fabulous hardy annual garden.

It is almost impossible to find the plants you want in the fall or early spring unless you start them yourself. If hardy annual plants are available at all on the retail market, it is seldom in the variety you want or at the correct planting

Twenty ¾-inch mini soil blocks with feverfew seedlings ready to be planted.

time for your garden. So starting your chosen seeds yourself is the way to go.

And yet, so many gardeners are daunted by the very idea of starting seeds for themselves. Why? Because, as little and innocent as those seeds appear, they are mysterious and unknown for the first-time seed-starter. The idea of starting your own is even more discouraging for a gardener who has already tried this and failed. The beautiful visions in the seed catalogs only make a mockery of the barren peat pots for those who have made an attempt with no success.

But seed starting can be easy once you learn a few basic ground rules to follow. And it can become downright addictive once you have your system in place and have a few successes under your belt.

Outdoors or Indoors?

Some plants prefer to have their seeds cast directly in the garden. Others should be started indoors and planted outside as a transplant. Still others are quite agreeable and can go either way – started indoors or cast directly in the garden. Learning the best planting method for any particular seed is the first step to success. The seed variety you are planting determines how best to plant.

With this bit of knowledge, you can choose which seeds to grow based on how you prefer to start seeds. Those who don't want to venture into starting seeds indoors can select seeds that prefer being cast directly in the garden. Those who are hooked on planting indoors can choose the seeds that thrive when that method is used.

Chapter 5 gave the preferred starting method for each of the 30 flowers profiled in this book. To learn about seeds for plants not mentioned, simply type the seed name along with "sowing instructions" into an online search engine for numerous results.

A bed of bupleurum in very early spring. Seeds were sown directly in the garden the previous fall. Bed and pathways mulched with a combination of straw and leaves.

Getting Started with Seeds

After determining if a particular seed should be started indoors or outdoors, the next natural step is to provide what it needs to sprout into a strong baby plant. By providing what a seed needs, you control how fast the seed sprouts, how many seeds will sprout, and how the seedlings will grow.

Start with live seeds. Buying from a reputable seed source ensures that the seeds are handled and stored in a way that preserves seed vitality. Starting with dead seeds is often the culprit in squashing the dreams of would-be stellar seed starters.

Planting and starting the seeds at the right time. This is essential. Timing is not so important in getting the seed to sprout, but it is crucial for the plant to perform to its full potential once it is in the garden. There is a window of opportunity that can close for that particular plant. If spring arrives and you haven't started the snapdragon seeds yet, for example, your best choice is to store the seeds away for next season. Storing in a cool, dark, low-humidity spot is best.

Lisianthus.

A perfect way to handle your seeds is to place them in a brown lunch bag, fold it closed and paper clip the bag to your calendar on the month you should plant them.

Do you cover the seed with soil or not? If the specifics are not on your seed packet as to whether to cover the seed with soil or not, find out before you plant. One of the leading causes of seed-starting failure is planting the seed too deeply. A seed has a pre-determined amount of food, strength and time to sprout. If it is planted too deeply, the seed runs out of steam before it can pop through the soil.

If the planting instructions say it needs light to germinate, place the seed firmly on the surface and do not cover. If it needs darkness to germinate, cover with ¼ - ½ inch of soil. Refer to Chapter 5 for this information on each of the flowers included in this book.

Planting Seeds Directly in the Garden

1. Prepare the soil (refer to Chapter 4) and smooth the surface flat.

2. To allow your flower seeds the same sprouting advantage as the weed seeds that naturally occur in all soils, you want to be certain that they all start to grow at the same time. Sometimes we give the weed seeds a head start simply because of our timing.

   Example: you prepare your soil today and plan to plant the seeds on another day. This means by the time you plant the flower seeds, the weed seeds are already ahead of them in sprouting and growing. The weeds easily overtake the flower seedlings you were hoping for. To even the playing field between your flower seeds and the weed seeds sprouting, use a hoe or rake to rough up the top 2 inches of soil before you plant. This will eliminate any germinating weed seedlings if there is a time lapse between preparing and planting

3. Using your hand or tool, make a trough or depression where you are going to plant seeds. This can be either in a straight line for a row garden or as a spread-open handprint impression in a grouping 10-12 inches apart for a mass landscape planting.

4. Plant a seed every 2-3 inches; sometimes this can be difficult with tiny seeds like poppies. Placing a few seeds in the palm of your hand makes it easier to just pick up one or two at a time. You should be planting two to three times the number of seeds that you want growing in the garden. Cover or leave uncovered according to instructions. For do-not-cover seeds, drop the seed in its spot and then gently firm

Dropping seeds into trough.

in by pressing with your hand. For cover seeds, drop the seed in its spot and then push about ¼ - ½ inch of soil to cover the seed.

Firming seed into soil for maximum contact.

5. Mark the planting. We all think we will remember, but rarely does it prove to be the case! Take a plastic picnic knife and

Marked handprint planting depression. Plant seeds within handprint for easy ID and also to gather water.

with a permanent garden marker write what flower it is and the date planted. Place a knife at either end of a straight row planting and a knife in the middle of each handprint for a mass planting. The knives will show you where your seedlings are as they begin to sprout along with random weeds.

6. Until all the seeds sprout, the seedbed may need to be watered once or twice daily if it is sunny and windy. Those watering chores can be reduced to every other day or so if you cover the seedbed with a floating row

Seedbed covered with a floating row cover between watering and hoeing chores. This provides moisture retention and protection from varmints like squirrels and birds.

cover. This is what we do on our farm to retain moisture and to protect seeds and seedlings from squirrels, rabbits and the like. *Watering tip:* Only water the troughs that your seeds are planted in. Watering the whole bed waters the weed seeds also.

7. The easiest way to prevent weeds is to stop the weed seeds from even sprouting in the seedbed. Pull back the row cover weekly and run a gardening hoe throughout the bed, except for where your plastic markers are indicating you planted the seeds. This will eliminate weed seeds that are preparing to sprout just like your flower seeds. This easy weekly chore will stack the odds in favor of your flower seeds' growth

over the weed seeds. Be sure to re-cover with the floating row cover between chores.

8. When they have sprouted, feed your seedlings with organic liquid fertilizer according to directions. This helps them to reach the size to be mulched as soon as possible. Continue feeding throughout the growing season.

9. Perhaps one of the most painful chores for a gardener to perform is thinning the seedlings once they have reached 4-6 inches tall. It's hard to pull out or cut down your beautiful plant babies! But to ensure the health and growth of your garden, you must give each seedling the room it needs to grow, eat and breathe.

Weekly, use a hoe to run throughout the bed except where markers indicate seeds are planted.

Thinning bells of Ireland seedlings according to the suggested spacing

Depending on the seed variety and the growing conditions, this chore can be done 6-16 weeks following the planting of seeds. We plant more seeds than needed, with the notion that not all seeds sprout for many reasons. Because we want a full, abundant garden, we plant with these failures in mind. Following thinning, run the garden hoe throughout the bed in preparation to mulch.

10. Mulching the garden thoroughly once your seedlings have reached 4-6 inches is the key to enjoying the blooming season of the garden. It will not only dress up the garden, but, more importantly, it will prevent the growth of weeds, saving you so much work in the weeding department.

    Use any organic mulch matter available to you, including, but not limited to: shredded leaves, bark, bale straw, compost, or pine straw. Weed prevention is not so dependent on what you use, but by how deeply it is applied. The goal is to cover the soil surface with at least 4-6 inches of mulch once the garden is mature. Apply mulch in a manner that does not smother the seedlings, yet is deep enough to prevent light from reaching the soil surface – light is what helps weed seeds to sprout. Top off mulch as your plants grow, if needed. For more on weed prevention and mulching the garden, see Chapter 8.

Touching up the mulch before netting the bed.

Starting Seeds Indoors

One of the greatest joys of a hardy annual garden is starting seeds indoors in the midst of the heat of summer and again during the dead of winter. On our farm, seed starting for fall plantings begins during the hottest time of summer, July and August. In January and February, when the ground is frozen and the winds are blowing winter into its glory, little baby plants are being born and stretching towards grow lights, trying to grow up in time for early spring plantings. Tending baby plants in the throes of extreme seasons sustains our

Three week old feverfew seedlings in mini soil blocks.

need to garden and is a reminder that spring is just around the corner.

Here on our farm, we prefer starting seeds indoors over planting directly in the garden, when given a choice. Starting inside is easier and it almost guarantees success in the garden. I find it easier to stand at a table to tend baby plants than to get down on my knees in the garden to do the same thing.

There are many different methods available to start seeds indoors: soil blocking, peat pots, plug trays and cowpots. The cowpots are made from composted cow manure; they are odorless and biodegradable. Some people recycle egg cartons or even paper towel roll tubes to plant in.

Soil blocking. The method I use is called soil blocking. We start all of the flower, herb, and vegetable plants this way on our farm. Soil blocks are small blocks of compressed soil that are made with a tool called a soil blocker. It is a method that has been used by the Dutch and English to start seeds for decades. I have been using it since 1998 with tremendous success. My initial attraction to this method was how little space you needed to start many plants and how easy it is to water the self-contained trays. These reasons make it perfect for the home gardener. Soil-blocking eliminates the need for buying and storing any containers other than re-usable trays.

I find that seedlings grown in soil bocks are more robust than those grown by other methods. They do not suffer from transplant shock and they also fruit and flower earlier. Since they tend to grow a bit quicker, they do not have to stay indoors as long as other seedlings.

Ten-day-old feverfew seedlings.

⚘ About Soil Blocking ⚘

There are several sizes of soil blockers available: the ¾-inch mini blocker makes 20 to a cluster; the 1½-inch blocker makes 5 to a cluster; the 2-inch blocker makes 4 to a cluster; and there is a jumbo 4-inch single blocker.

I use the ¾-inch mini blocker almost exclusively on our farm. Two sets of these mini clusters fit on a 5x7-inch tray – 40 plants. The only time we go larger is when the actual seed is too large for the mini blocker, such as sweet pea seeds, and then I use the 2-inch blocker. We plant seeds, as seen in the following pages, and grow them in that ¾-inch block until they are planted outdoors in the garden. The key to the success and the space-thriftiness of the mini blocker is not to start seeds too early. The garden should be waiting to receive them the moment they are large enough. Hanging around waiting for better planting conditions leads to overgrown transplants growing out of the blocks.

Here are the steps I follow to make and plant seeds with soil blocks:

1. *Organic blocking mix.* Blocking mix differs from most seed-starting and potting mixes because the mix needs to hold and bind together, instead of being loose and crumbly. The recipe listed below will make

2-inch soil blocker, inserts for the 2-inch blocker, and the ¾-inch mini soil blocker.

approximately 600 of the mini ¾-inch individual blocks. A kitty litter box-type tub works well to mix in. The Ready-to-Use Blocking Mix and nutrients are available from suppliers listed in Appendix C. Mix together the following:

- 16 cups of sifted peat moss or coco fiber
- 4 cups of sifted compost
- ¼ cup of greensand
- ¼ cup of rock phosphate powder

When ready to make the blocks, add approximately 6-7 cups of water to the recipe. Wet the entire recipe even if you aren't going to use it all at this time. I find it easier to make the blocks when I have a nice mound of soil to work in. Any excess can be dried out and re-wet for future use. If you experience trouble getting the blocks to deploy from the blocker, it is normally because the mix is too dry. The consistency that works best is very moist, but with no water standing in the tray after mixing.

2. How to make soil blocks:

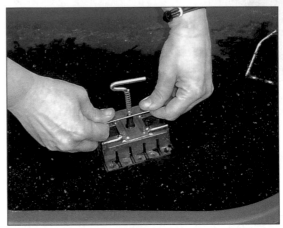

Holding the stationary bar of the soil blocker, push it into the mound of blocking mix to fill the chambers. I do this twice to ensure a firm block.

To deploy the blocks, push the plunger while lifting the blocker an inch or two off of the tray.

Place a few seeds in an aluminum seed pan; using a toothpick moistened with saliva, pick up and place one seed on each block. Aluminum has no static cling and saliva is much stickier than water. This method makes quick and easy work out of planting tens of thousands of seeds on our farm each year.

To water without damaging the blocks, pour water into the tray, not over the blocks, to be absorbed. Any excess water left standing after a couple of minutes can be carefully poured out.

3. How to plant ¾-inch mini blocks. Pick up the entire cluster and place on your hand, break apart the blocks as you plant. It is quick and easy.

For a Larger Transplant:

When a larger plant is desired for transplanting to the garden, it is easy to move the mini block seedling up into a 2-inch block for continued growth. This is especially helpful for those with a shorter growing season where there is a real need for a more mature transplant. Make the 2-inch blocks with the inserts installed. The insert creates a perfect size hole to drop the mini block into. Gently compress to snug in and the roots will continue to grow into the larger block.

What Your Seeds Need to Sprout Indoors

Soil blocks are placed on a seedling heat mat to encourage a speedier and more consistent sprouting.

Once 50% of the seeds have sprouted, move from heat to light. Seedlings require 16 hours of light a day to grow into healthy transplants.

Seedlings should be moved outdoors to harden off under a carport about one week before planting in the garden.

Newly planted sweet pea vines covered with a floating row cover to offer protection while they become established.

Regardless of the method you choose to start your seeds indoors, your success will hinge on providing the warmth, light and food the seeds need to sprout and grow.

- Once planted indoors, seeds need a degree of warmth to get started. Most seeds sprout at 70-85 degrees; most home temperatures are about 70 degrees. The mass of soil your seeds are planted in is about 15-20 degrees cooler than the surrounding air temperature, so 70-degree house equals 55-degree soil. This is a common reason for seed-starting failure indoors – the seeds just aren't warm enough.

A seed-starting heat mat will warm the soil and encourage a higher number of seeds to sprout, and they will do so quickly and more evenly. Once 50% of the seeds sprout, move from the heat mat to light. Using a seed-starting heat mat also helps to prevent damping off, a fungus that attacks seedlings as a result of cool, moist soil. When you find young seedlings lying down, and it appears they have been pinched at the base, this is called damping off.

A special note about temperature:
To provide the 70-degree temperature preferred by some, place a cookie-baking cooling rack on top of the seed-starting heat mat to create an air space between the seedling container and the actual mat. This cools it down a bit for these cool-season lovers.

- Allow the soil to almost dry out between watering, which is often needed daily.

- Provide 16 hours of light a day to grow strong, healthy and stocky transplants. When they don't receive the required amount of light, they stretch into tall, lengthy plants with faded, spindly foliage. Strong, healthy plants live on to produce more flowers and fruit and are naturally more disease- and pest-resistant.

- A good source of food provides fuel for your seedling to develop naturally into a strong transplant. We prefer to use an organic seaweed/fish type fertilizer; use according to directions. A slow, steady supply of food enriches growth and helps the plant to become more self-sustaining with each application.

- Planting transplants outdoors is generally done when the plants reach 4-6 inches. How fast your seedlings grow depends on the growing environment you provide. In a warm room, seedlings will grow faster; cooler conditions will slow them down. We find that seedlings grow faster in soil blocks and in general, most of our plants go to the garden at 3-4 weeks old.

  Once the seedlings are 2-3 inches tall, we move them outdoors into a protected spot. We gradually introduce them into full sun and wind before planting out in the garden. This period of transition is called hardening off. It provides time for the tender plants to be acclimated to the outdoors. We continue this transition by placing a floating row cover immediately over the seedlings once they are planted in the garden. We leave the row cover for 10-14 days until the plants are well established. The row cover also protects from birds, rabbits, deer and drying wind.

- To plant the transplants in the garden: prepare the soil (see Chapter 4) and smooth the surface flat. You can mulch immediately. I prefer to mulch first, and then plant the baby plants into the mulched garden. This prevents smashing or smothering the transplants during the task of mulching. See Chapter 7 for suggestions on mulching and weed prevention.

Starting from seed gives you not only more choices for your garden, but also an avenue for becoming invested in your garden from the very beginning. Once your first baby plant is born from seed and grows into a plant that produces a flower, you will understand. From that time on, your dreams will be all about what seeds you can start next!

Ammi majus 'Queen of Africa'

Seven

How to Include Hardy Annuals in Your Garden

Learn from your garden – she sends signs all the time; you just have to take notice. Living with hardy annuals in the garden has been my best teacher. I remember rooting around in the garden in the fall of my second year growing commercially and finding the pleasant surprise of self-sown bupleurum and *Ammi* baby seedlings scattered about. Realizing when the flowers chose to sprout on their own in my garden helped me to tweak when I should sow hardy annual seeds in the future. I keep on learning.

Rudbeckia 'Indian Summer' and *Ammi visnaga* 'Green Mist' are happy garden companions that have self-sown themselves as neighbors.

In the Landscape and Containers

Hardy annuals are an excellent source of blooms for the landscape and in containers. Some of the early bloomers are especially appreciated in the area of the landscape that you frequent, like the bed at the door used every day. A planting of sweet William comes to mind when I think of early flowers. It is so hardy that it is possible for many regions to plant in the fall, pushing the plants into bloom even earlier. The 'Sweet' variety is one of the first bloomers in our garden, making it a real treat to enjoy.

To keep the landscape planting blooming longer, deadhead weekly. Following the suggested removal of old blooms will keep the plant producing long after plantings that are not deadheaded. This chore should be considered when selecting the spot to plant; you are more likely to do it if you have easy access.

Hardy annuals, such as pansies, are long-time favorites for containers. Many of the hardy annuals in this book are perfect companions to complete a container. The rule I follow is to use the very largest container possible for maximum root growth and lowest daily maintenance. I am willing to try any plant that has a mature size of less than 36". This has revealed some real winners and also a couple of not-so-great choices. Think outside the box for the sake of a beautiful spring container!

Spring blooming hardy annuals are the perfect bouquet companions to other flowers blooming in your garden. Pictured: Snapdragons 'Rocket', larkspur 'Sublime', bachelor button 'Blue Boy', along with a few white peonies.

A Cutting Garden

The spring cutting garden can be the pot of gold at the end of a long, cold winter. Growing a small designated cutting garden is so satisfying. The garden's sole purpose is to provide fresh-cut flowers for your table and to share with friends.

The suggested size of this garden is quite manageable. A 3'x10'garden is large enough to produce an abundance of cut flowers, especially when you tend it as a cutting garden. The size alone is the beginning of success because it concentrates the preparation, planting, and tending to one small spot. For those thinking this bed too small, read on before going larger! Consider the force that drives a cutting garden.

The lifeline of a cutting garden is harvesting all the flowers that are opening on a regular schedule. A spring garden will surprise you with how fast flowers develop from just a shoot to open blooms. Harvesting the flowers on a regular schedule will keep the garden producing a continuous harvest of fresh flowers. This means that the spring garden may require a more frequent harvest than the summer or fall cutting garden.

The sheer abundance that a garden produces when you tend it as a cutting garden is unexpected, which can actually bring about the demise of the cutting garden. There are so many flowers at each cutting that we don't take time to cut them all. We begin leaving open flowers in the garden since we have more than we need, and the garden in turn stops producing new stems because the old stems are still hanging around. To make matters worse, you may neglect going out and cutting new flowers, because the ones you gathered last week are still so pretty in the vase. Flowers fresh from the home garden last longer than flowers from the store, and you are even less likely to go out and cut emerging new blooms.

Keeping the cutting garden small is the first step to success. You want to be able to stay on top of the harvesting. This is crucial to every garden, whether it is yielding flowers, vegetables or herbs. You must harvest on a regular basis – not just when you need the bounty. While many gardeners successfully follow the steps to grow a cutting garden, their gardens fail because they do not harvest as needed to keep it producing throughout the season.

❧ Steps to Success ❧

- **Suggested plants:** The flowers in this suggested cutting garden are ones I prefer to start indoors. You can set the bed up while they are inside under a grow light. Start these seeds indoors at the proper time for your winter hardiness zone and plant outdoors accordingly. See Chapter 6.

- **Location of the garden:** Choose a site with 6-8 hours of full sun; late afternoon shade is appreciated and will prolong spring blooming. Locate out of sight from inside your home. If you can enjoy how this garden looks from the kitchen window, you will be loath to ruin the sight by cutting off all the

3"x 10" Cutting Bed

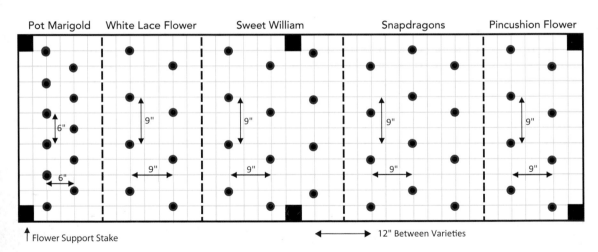

↑ Flower Support Stake   ◄─────► 12" Between Varieties

This transplanted cutting garden includes: Pot marigolds 'Pacific Beauties Series' mixed colors, height 24"; white lace flower, height 24"; sweet William 'Amazon', height 24"-30"; snapdragons 'Rocket' mixed colors, height 36"; pincushion flower 'Fire King', 'Blue Cockade', or 'Black Knight,', height 24"-36". Space as indicated with garden stakes to support the flower support netting.

blooms. The perfect location in most yards is where you don't landscape, for the very reason that you can't see it. This may be behind a garage or along the far side of the house. Consider where your water source is located. This garden will need frequent watering when newly planted and then one inch a week to keep the blooms coming.

A bed of snapdragons 'Opus' mixed colors with flower support netting installed – they will remain standing through rain and wind.

- **Preparing the bed:** Follow the "getting started" steps in Chapter 4 to prepare your soil.

- **Setting up for low-maintenance:** Because you are planting transplants in this garden, the bed can be mulched before planting. Follow the suggested steps in Chapter 8 for covering the bed with biodegradable mulch film or several layers of newspaper first, then topping off with mulch. This will set the bed up for practically a weed-free season and it will have excellent moisture retention. Plant the transplant through the mulch by punching a hole in the film or newspaper and tucking it into the soil.

- **Cover while getting established:** The shape of this flower bed is perfect for being easily covered with a floating row cover. Leave the cover on for 10-14 days after planting. For fall and winter plantings, the cover can be left on longer if desired. Remove the cover temporarily for hand watering and weeding chores.

- **Keep the flowers tall and straight:** It is essential to support the tall stems of cutting garden flowers to prevent them from tumbling to the ground. There is nothing more disappointing after all the work than to watch a burst of torrential rain pound the flowers to the ground. Tumbling is prevented with flower support netting. Install the netting in very early spring after discontinuing the use of a floating row cover. It is easiest to put in while the plants are young and still short. When placed at this time, the netting virtually disappears as the plants grow up through it. This suggested garden has plants of varying heights and has been laid out in the bed with this in mind – shorter maturity heights at one end with the tallest at the opposite end. The netting is suspended over the bed using strong garden stakes. While this bed appears very innocent when young, the taller varieties can be very heavy once mature and loaded with blooms, so use strong stakes. Six stakes placed as seen in the diagram are recommended for this size garden. The netting should rest on the stake at a height of about halfway up the mature plant. For example, if the plant is 30" when mature, netting should be at 15". Because this is a mixed bed, I would place the netting at 12-15 inches at the shorter plants end and slightly higher at the other end. It is easier to pull netting up if needed instead of pushing it down once the plants begin growing through.

- **Waiting for the blooms:** After the bed is netted we literally just wait for the plants to start blooming. For the best growth and re-bloom, feed your plants with liquid organic fertilizer according to directions. This is in addition to the dry organic fertilizer

mixed in during preparation. Because of the high demand on these performance plants, they will need all the natural nutrients possible. When you meet the nutrient needs, they will continue to produce more stems and also bigger flowers through the season.

- **Harvesting:** What has helped me the most with harvesting regularly is making a date with the garden, and sticking to it. If you plan to cut twice a week, mark your calendar for ten minutes in the garden every Monday and Friday. It might be in the morning or right before dusk – both have advantages, with the middle of the day being the absolute last option. Once you get into the habit, it will come naturally. While harvesting, you will come across flowers that are blemished or unusable. Be sure to cut them and toss them in the compost heap. Or you can do as we do, and drop them in the pathway to become part of our pathway lasagna compost. We remove any foliage from the stem that falls below 6-8 inches from the bloom. The more foliage removed, the less stress on the stem. Following the suggested stage of when to harvest (in Chapter 5), is key to the longest-lasting and most pristine blooms. The optimal time to harvest a cut

Stages to Harvest. 1. Pincushion flower: any time, from a textured button to when ⅓ of the tiny flowers are open. 2. Sweet William: when ⅓ of the flowers are open. 3. Snapdragons: as the first bottom flower opens. 4. Bupleurum: any time after more than half of the tiny blooms are open.

flower is when it is as early in the opening stage as possible, while still mature enough to continue opening indoors. This prevents damage to the blossoms from chewing insects that also soil the flowers, leaving spots (ick!). It minimizes damage from weather conditions such as rain.

- **Harvest gear:** To make a nice clean cut while harvesting, use a sharp bypass shear (see Appendix C for information and sources). Placing the flower stems into a clean container filled with clean water and fresh-cut-flower food is greatly undervalued – more on this later. Water with flower food in it is called "conditioned water."

The container you harvest into and the ultimate vase they land in should be clean enough that you would be willing to drink water from it. When you use a dirty container, the water residue and scum in it are just waiting for you to fill it with water. That very minute, the whole lifecycle of bacteria that rots flowers is jumpstarted. If your container is clean, you delay that bacteria process, adding time to your vase life.

- **Making the cut:** Go to the garden with your clean harvest container filled with conditioned water. Familiarize yourself with where to make the suggested cut on specific flowers from Chapter 5. This is especially important for the first cut, because it sets the plant up for branching for the rest of the season. Remember, you are making the actual cut where the plant needs it to grow more strong stems in the future – not just cutting the stem the length you need for the vase.

- **Help your cut flowers to last longer:** What should you put in the water? Fresh-cut-flower food does make a difference in how long your flowers last in a vase. The misunderstanding that "cut-flower food doesn't make a difference" has come from the high use of imported flowers. Before these flowers reach the vases they have traveled from afar and for many days. Often they are shipped dry in boxes, causing many of these flower stems to be clogged. Clogged stems cannot drink water when they finally get it, so they cannot in fact reap the many benefits from cut-flower food. This is not true with home-grown flowers. Your flowers will never be without water to clog and stress the stems.

When you plunge your freshly-harvested garden flowers into a container full of clean water with cut-flower food in it, it will keep the water clean, provide food for continued development of buds and prevent conditions that can lead to clogged stems. Allowing your flowers to rest for at least 4 hours after they have been cut is recommended. This helps them to recover from literally having their lifeline cut and to rehydrate after the loss they've experienced. After making your bouquet, place it in a vase with fresh water and cut-flower food. Monitor the water level of your vase daily; fresh garden flowers tend to guzzle water. Every 2-3 days, replenish or replace water, trimming one to two inches from the stems before replacing in the vase.

The Self-Appointed Garden

The self-appointed garden includes those hardy annual plants that self-sow their seeds in the garden to return in the coming years. It is like a treasure hunt in the garden and the adjoining areas in early spring, looking for those seedlings that have magically appeared. To think that the plants were so happy in my garden that they chose to return is inspiring!

The secret to including these self-sowing plants in your garden is to consider not only where you are planting them now, but also that this is where they will freely re-seed in coming years. My suggestion is to have a designated garden or area of the garden for the self-sowers. This allows you to manage the frequent problem of crowding of the self-sown seedlings.

While these little seedlings do show up on their own power in the garden in the years to come, you will need to help them to grow into healthy members of the garden. Strong, healthy plants will grow on to produce beautiful blooms that lead to seeds for the next year's crop.

Thinning or transplanting the seedlings to suggested spacing is crucial to the survival of this stand of plants in the garden. Transplanting self-sown seedlings should be done when the seedlings are very small for best results. I like to use a garden scoop for this job because it will hold a nice, deep clump of soil surrounding the seedling roots. Transplant a small cluster of seedlings together without thinning them at this point. After planting

Transplanting self-sown seedlings. 1. Use a scoop to get as much soil as possible around roots. 2. Gather several seedling clusters to transplant. 3. Make a similar size hole to place the transplant into to prevent root damage. 4. Gently firm the transplant in the hole to eliminate any air pockets.

and allowing them to recover for a few days, continue to thin by pulling the excess seedlings in the clump, leaving the strongest as the transplant.

To remove excess crowded seedlings, I do a little hand pulling, then use the stand-up or hand garden hoe for quick and easy removal. First, pull by hand those seedlings that are very closely clustered to the seedling you want to save. Then, run the hoe throughout the bed, as suggested in Chapter 8, removing the remaining unwanted seedlings.

Once the seedlings are thinned, mulch the garden to discourage weed seeds from sprouting. Feed the plants using organic liquid fertilizer according to directions. To encourage next season's seeds to readily germinate, do not mulch deeply. The seeds that are self-sown by the plants will need to make some contact with soil, so no more than 1-2 inches of mulch in this garden.

Reaping What You Sow

These steps may seem like just motions to go through in your garden. However, this is where the tending and cultivating really come alive. Enjoying the landscape and garden on cool mornings, deadheading the pansies, and discovering little seedlings that have sudden grown up into big plants is what spring is all about in a garden. This anticipation and discovery keeps us coming back to the garden during this season of hope and new life. The best part: so much is already happening in your garden while other folks are just dreaming of when they can plant!

Fabulous Fall-Winter-Spring Container
Tulips and Pansies

This is an easy keeper container that is beautiful from fall through spring. The pansies provide color from fall throughout winter. In spring the tulips emerge for the grand finale.

Shopping List:

Minimum container size: 14" wide, 10" deep
Potting soil with slow-release fertilizer
For a 14"-wide pot: 30 tulip bulbs and five 6" pots of pansies

How-to:

- Fill the container to 3"-4" with potting soil.
- Place tulips bulbs as close as eggs in a carton in the container
- Fill the container to $^2/_3$ full with soil and firm in.
- Place the pansies in the container, fill in with soil. The finished soil level should be 1 inch below the container rim.
- Water very well.
- When spring arrives and the tulips pop through – surprise!

Eight

FINISHING TOUCHES FOR EASY KEEPING

I f anyone has invented a maintenance-free garden, I haven't heard of it. But there are certainly steps you can take to minimize maintenance. When that happens, you will spend more and more time enjoying your garden. With a short chore list, you can embark on the wonderful process of tending and cultivating the garden – which makes it such a pleasure.

In this chapter I'll share with you how to minimize chores, maximize healthy plants, and get the very most from every square foot of space you garden.

During my first years as a flower farmer, I can remember feeling overwhelmed and

A fall-planted hardy annual garden in mid-April, just waiting for the flowers to start blooming. It is set-up for a season of low maintenance.

even desperate for relief at times. It seemed as though there just wasn't enough of me to go around. I went to bed each night with more on the to-do list than I had when I began the day. This problem quickly snowballed out of control. In a garden and on a farm, the chores you don't get to tend to keep growing into bigger jobs – bigger than when you first put them on the chore list. Get the idea? Your chores mushroom into even more work you don't have time to do.

How to garden smart

Some words of wisdom from a neighbor – a career farmer himself – sparked my journey to gardening "smarter" instead of "harder." He shared with me that he had as many chores to do the day he retired from farming as the day he began, 50 years before. It is the nature of tending a living thing – the work is never done. He explained that figuring out how to eliminate the need for some of the chores is the only way to be free of the heavy load. He finished by reminding me that it is this tending to a living, growing thing that draws us to it in the first place.

This conversation took place many years ago in the hot afternoon sun along my garden fence. Though we were farmers from two totally different farming worlds, it opened the window to the method of gardening I practice today. What I have come to learn through the years since then reinforces this ideology and continues to drive organic gardening on my farm. Growing strong, healthy plants eliminates the need for the chores and treatments associated with herbicides and pesticides. And weeding is a small task when you prevent weeds from ever sprouting in the first place. This kind of thinking is really simple and smart, when you consider it.

Now I want to give you the steps I follow in our gardens that minimize our chores, help our plants be their healthiest, and encourage every square foot of space to do its most for us. Some are common garden practices and others I learned through trials and frustration. Those lessons are sometimes the sweetest.

I have outlined how to care for the direct-sown and transplanted garden here. The "how-to" steps are expanded on the following pages.

Caring for the Direct-Sown Garden

1. Uncovering direct sown garden in early spring; 2. Hand pulling some weeds; 3.Using a hand hoe to remove several unwanted seedlings with one pull; 4. Thinned seedlings mulched and ready to grow.

Perhaps the most important step I have learned with a direct-sown garden is this: get the weeds when they are developing. A just-developing weed has a tiny root system – that bigger weed has deeper, stronger roots and is robbing your plant of food and water.

- Do not allow the seed bed to dry out during the sprouting stage.
- After the seeds have sprouted, begin feeding with organic liquid fertilizer according to directions.

- Seedlings started directly in the garden in fall normally don't require winter hoeing chores once the temperatures drop into the 40s and below.
- The job most on my mind in early spring is to thin seedlings, run a hoe through the bed and mulch.
- If you are using flower support netting, it can be installed any time after the use of floating row cover has been discontinued and the bed is mulched.

⋇ Caring for the Transplanted Garden ⋇

Many care steps are eliminated when you plant transplants in the garden instead of planting seeds directly in the garden.

- For the easiest transplanting, mulch the bed before planting.
- Directly after planting, water the plants using organic liquid fertilizer, following directions. Continue feeding throughout the growing season.

- The first 14 days after planting, pay close attention to the plants so that they do not dry out. One inch of water weekly is necessary for continued healthy growth. Covering with a floating row cover will retain moisture and reduce watering chores.
- Re-cover the transplants with the floating row cover between chores.
- If flower support netting is used, it can be installed any time after the use of floating row cover has been discontinued.

Hoeing: Keep the Garden Weed Free

The stand-up hoe. The stand-up garden hoe has gotten a bad rap. That is due to the poor design of most of the hoes being used in gardens. The hoes that farmers use are efficient and effortless to use. They eliminate developing weeds in a way that does not bring fresh weed seeds up to the surface, because they do not dig deep into the soil. My favorite is the 6-inch trapezoid hoe. I find it most versatile for removing developing weeds as well as larger established weeds. The key feature of a long-handled garden hoe is the angle of the blade to the handle. When the blade is flat on the ground, the handle should be upright, as pictured. This allows you to stand up straight, hold the handle with your thumbs up, positioning the handle fairly close to your body while you pull the hoe blade through the top 1-2 inches of soil. Imagine slicing a stick of butter lengthwise by pulling a warm knife through the length of the stick – that is how the hoe blade should move through the soil. By only disturbing the top couple of inches of soil, the supply of weed seeds on the surface diminishes each time you hoe. This reduces the number of sprouting weed seedlings.

The correct position to hoe is standing upright, thumbs up on the handle, blade flat on the ground, and pulling the hoe blade through the top 1-2 inches of soil. Effortless and efficient weed removal.

The hand hoe. The hand hoe I use is called a Japanese grass weeder. For some jobs, I just prefer to be down on the ground for a closer look when hoeing. Thinning seedlings is one of those jobs. This hoe head is 4 inches wide so I can make pulls across a row of seedlings to be thinned and remove several seedlings with one pull. Then I fine tune the spacing with hand pulling. This is especially useful when seeds have been sown thickly, as I recommend with bells of Ireland. The hand hoe may also be used for general weeding. Note that this blade works the same as the stand-up version – with the blade flat on the ground and moving 1-2 inches below the surface.

With each passing week, there will be fewer and fewer weed seeds on the surface to sprout, if you move your sharp hoe blade through the soil like a razor (instead of chopping with it like an ax). The best advice with weeding: get the weeds when they are young and small – it is effortless to hoe a bed when weed seeds are barely visible or just sprouting. Tough, mature weeds are quite another story.

Mulch: the Soil's Life Preserver

Using biodegradable film or layers of newspaper helps to prevent weeds from sprouting. Covering all the soil in a garden prevents weeds, keeps soil cooler and retains moisture.

Mulching is so much more than a decorative touch to finish off the garden. Mulch retains moisture, cools the soil in summer, and provides habitat for many beneficial creatures above and below the soil.

Mulch also suppresses weeds naturally when applied at the right time. Here are some steps I follow in my garden when mulching for weed prevention:

• **Never leave soil bare – not even for a few days.** Those few days in the sun are just what most annual weed seeds have been waiting for. They will pop out of the ground in no time. By covering the soil with mulch right away after working the soil, you will prevent most annual weeds from ever being born.

- **Mulch pathways deeply.** If you have garden pathways or open areas with no plants, mulch deeper than when mulching within a planted area. We mulch our garden pathways 8-10 inches with leaves and straw.

- **Use biodegradable mulch film or newspaper under mulch.** A layer of film or several layers of newspaper beneath mulch blocks light from getting to the soil. Mulch does not need to be as deep when you do this. Both break down over time and are very easy to pop a hole in to plant through. The black film also has the added benefit of warming the soil when not covered with mulch.

Added Protection: Floating Row Cover

Floating row cover offers your seeds and plants protection from wind, cold temperatures, hot sun, and hungry, marauding critters. The breathable cloth provides excellent moisture retention because it protects from drying wind and hot sun, thereby reducing watering chores. One of my favorite uses is for preventing damage from birds, squirrels, rabbits and deer. The animals don't seem to realize anything is under the cloth, so they totally disregard it. Cover new plantings of seeds until they have sprouted and are large enough to be mulched. Cover transplants for 14 days or longer, until the transplants are well-established. The light

Floating row cover protects a bed from drying wind, birds, squirrels, rabbits and deer.

weight cover allows 85% of the sunlight to pass through. Air and rain also pass through. With row cover, you can count on about a 4-degree temperature advantage.

Use heavy objects like rocks or milk jugs of water to hold the covers down in the garden. If hand watering the bed, push back the cover to do so. The cover can be laid directly on the plants and seedbeds, or hooped using #9 wire or ½-inch pex PVC flexible pipe for long term cover use. In an effort to get the absolutely earliest blooms, and also for deer protection, I leave the covers on fall and winter plantings until very early spring. Covers are useable from year to year. Store out of weather when not in use.

❧ Microclimates ❧

A microclimate is a spot where conditions are different from the surrounding area. It can be naturally occurring or you can create one (see page 38). It may offer a more hospitable growing condition such as protection from winds or the hot afternoon sun. Here on my farm we have very strong winds that give fall planting of hardy annuals a good beating all winter. So I create a microclimate using row covers. We hoop our plantings and cover the beds with floating row cover. Perhaps the most under-appreciated use of row cover is wind protection. Those little plants just thrive under cover – there is no wind to speak of, while the bright winter sun warms their roots. Covering plants to create this nice "microclimate" can also bring on earlier blooms.

A bed of snapdragons in early spring after spending winter under a row cover.

✂ Thinning Seedlings ✂

It might be hard for tender-hearted gardeners to do, but thinning your seedlings to the recommended spacing will produce more flowers and result in healthier, prettier plants. When seedlings are young and crowded, they may look healthy. However, when they grow up crowded, they must fight for water, air space, and nutrients – there will never be enough to go around. The result is a puny stand of plants that quickly fall victim to disease and pests because of their condition.

Thinning is easily done with a hoe and by hand. To prevent causing damage to the seedlings you are keeping, thin while the plants are small. It is a chore you might cringe to do – but be strong and do it to save the ship!

✂ Flower Support Netting and Trellising ✂

This plastic reusable netting supports plants that grow tall or have heavy flower heads. It is 6x6-inch white plastic mesh that is easily suspended over the plant using garden stakes. The netting height should rest at the midway mark of the mature plant size. Installing when the plants are young and short is best. As the plant grows up through the netting, it practically disappears from sight.

Sweet peas are a vining plant that needs support. Providing a trellis for the vines to climb will encourage them to grow upright keeping them more compact and easier to harvest from.

Growing sweet pea vines on a trellis makes harvesting and deadheading easy.

Feeding Your Plants

Providing nutrients will enhance your plant performance and provide a better crop. If you are using organic fertilizers, you will make your soil healthier in the process. In addition to the dry organic fertilizer mixed into the soil when getting started, I also use organic liquid seaweed and fish fertilizer. Mix and use according to directions. It can be poured on the soil as a drench and can also be sprinkled or sprayed on the foliage as a foliar feed, which I have found to be very beneficial to plants. It does have a smell, so I stop foliar feeding when I want to start harvesting flowers for cuts. With fall plantings, you can stop feeding during the cold temperatures of winter, to restart in early spring. This additional liquid feeding is not necessary for average performance, but if you are cutting from your plants or just want the biggest and best from them, they will need this boost of food to keep up the marathon of production.

Pulling It All together for Success

If you want to have a low-maintenance garden, you must set it up to be that way. That's the secret to liberating yourself from the never-ending chore list. Think of all the enjoyable ways to pass time in a garden: planting more plants, puttering around watching bugs (my favorite), or sitting among your flowers to read a book. These are all possibilities when you take a step back and make a plan. Think of what you want to do; gather the tools and supplies you need to do it with; and then when you do it, complete the job!

In my talks, I often share the way we survive on our busy flower farm and get it all done. We set our beds up as described and then leave them until they start blooming. The right tools and good timing can go a long way to preventing the need for some garden chores. That's the secret to easy keeping and organic gardening.

Nine

AND NOW... THE REWARDS!

As winter gives way to spring, a hardy annual garden comes alive. It's amazing to see this happen, especially after a long, harsh winter. The work of preparing and planting the hardy annual garden is just a faint memory. With the birds, the bugs, and little baby shoots sprouting from seedlings...ahhh. Now the garden is loaded with excitement and activity! There is still plenty of work to be done on my farm in spring, preparing to plant tender annual flowers for summer blooms and gearing up for the harvest to begin. But it's the solace of the hardy annual garden that ignites my passion for the season and beyond.

My love for spring may stem from an absence that has made my heart grow fonder. Whatever the reason, for me, this season of new beginning takes first place in my garden.

My hardy annual garden in early April, on the verge of bursting into bloom. Beds left to right: snapdragons, feverfew, and *Ammi visnaga*.

Reuniting with Spring Flowers

I live and garden in southeastern Virginia in plant hardiness zone 7. Along with most other gardeners living in areas with long, hot and humid summers, I had always been under the impression that we cannot grow many of the flowers in this book. It was a revelation to me that planting at the correct time would give me a robust plant performing in spring and into summer. Once discovered, this practice has made it possible for me to grow flowers I could only dream about before.

A beautiful bouquet that is delightful to the senses and the eye. Bells of Ireland, snapdragons, larkspur, bupleurum, *Ammi majus*, sweet William, and feverfew.

Perhaps here a beginning gardener has an advantage. The novice tends to grasp the idea of fall, winter and early spring planting of hardy annuals more readily than the more experienced gardener. The seasoned gardener typically has had firsthand experience attempting to grow these plants and failing miserably. It is hard to accept that it was just that the timing was off for planting. When planted at the correct time, hardy annuals thrive with minimal assistance and they face spring and summer with little difficulty. It seems too good to be true, especially for anyone who has already tried and failed.

The old gardening practice of planting hardy annuals in cool temperatures is being re-kindled. This is going to reunite gardeners with some of the greatest flowers to be grown in a garden. Many, like me, who garden in the middle to lower regions of the country, will have success with these flowers for the first time. Spring will never be the same.

✂ Sharing Flowers ✂

Sharing your cut flowers with others can be one of the greatest rewards of your garden. Even after all these years, there is always a thrill when I hand my flowers to others – whether it is to a customer of many years or to a friend given as a gift. People are simply in awe. It is not just the beauty, freshness and fragrance that overcomes them. The fact that I tended, nurtured and grew them literally sweeps them off their feet.

It is so easy to make bouquets to share. Having an outlet for the harvested flowers beyond your own needs will keep you out there harvesting – which keeps the flowers producing more blooms. Sharing cut flowers from your garden is an experience full of rewards for both receiver and giver.

Hardy annuals make beautiful standalone bouquets or mix beautifully with others flowers blooming in your garden.
1. Pot marigolds; 2. Black-eyed Susan, larkspur, feverfew, bupleurum, and lambada, with hydrangeas; 3. Snapdragons, dill, bupleurum, and yarrow; 4.Snapdragons, larkspur, and perennial peonies.

A Garden with a Purpose

One way we market our cut flowers is through a weekly subscription bouquet drop-off service. A few years ago, it turned out that I had four friends all going through cancer treatments at the same time. So I asked my sister, Suzanne, to make four extra bouquets for me to drop off to let them know we were thinking of them. I placed a bucket with flowers and a note on each porch that said, "Leave this bucket here each Monday, filled with water, and we will refill it with fresh blossoms and love just for you." What a meaningful season that was! Suzanne and I were the ones to receive the blessings. The cards, phone calls and porch hugs from these gals were overwhelming.

Since then, two of the four have lost their battles with cancer. At their services, their families could not stop talking about how much that small act of kindness meant to them and their lost loved ones. The joy those flowers brought had reached far beyond any expectation I ever imagined.

I learned there is something very special about giving a gift that you have grown and tended yourself. The gift of flowers from your own garden touches others in away nothing else does. One friend – since lost – would call each week to thank me and say, "I can't believe you grow these, I just sit and stare at them all day, and I think of you working in the garden."

Imagine my surprise when I was diagnosed with breast cancer the next year. I was fortunate; mine was detected early and treated with little discomfort. During the time I was recuperating, the idea for a special cutting garden was born in my mind. This garden would be pink to honor those who have had breast cancer and to raise awareness of the disease; after all, I was now the poster girl for early detection. Most of all, I wanted to continue the tradition of sharing the flowers from my garden. Sharing them created opportunities for conversations about early detection that I hoped would make a difference for someone else.

I had grown a pink warm-season tender annual cutting garden for several years. So the next natural step was to create a pink cutting garden of hardy annuals. This suggested garden includes plants that prefer to have their seeds sown directly in the garden. This means that the bed cannot be mulched until the seedlings have reached 4-6 inches. This bed, when happy, will replant itself for years to come.

Sowing these seeds will bring a bounty of spring blooms to share – truly a labor of love, joy, and hope!

Our pink garden includes: 1. Larkspur 'Sublime Pink'; 2. Corn cockle 'Pink Contessa'; 3. Bachelor buttons 'Boy Pinkie'; 4. Lambada; 5. Love-in-a-mist rose

Beneficial Creatures in the Garden

Good Bugs

While we tend to plan our gardens for beautiful displays and cut flowers, there is another very important reason to grow some of these early hardy annual bloomers: beneficial insects. Gardeners may be familiar with the popular ladybug and honeybee, but there are many other beneficial insects as well. These good guys can do everything from pollinating your plants to gobbling up the harmful insects that damage your plants. They will happily come to live and work in the garden if you set your garden up to provide what they need.

If I had to choose one group of flowers to attract beneficial insects to my garden, it would be hardy annuals. Many of these flowers are nectar-rich and offer early blooms when few others are available; and many of the flowers are composed of tightly packed clusters of little flowers – a favorite of many beneficial insects. Lots of these guys have tiny mouths so they need tiny flowers to eat from.

Our farm has a strong population of beneficial insects. Our enticing spring garden starts early with nectar-rich bachelor buttons and pot marigolds, with members of the *umbellifers* family joining in soon after. The *umbellifers* are all packed with clusters of tiny flowers; *Ammi majus*, *Ammi visnaga*, bupleurum, dill, false Queen Anne's lace, white lace flower, and yarrow, and are very attractive to beneficial insects. This spring garden is so rich that it not only attracts the good guys, it encourages them to hang around and raise babies.

Native pollinators are a part of our beneficial insect family. These pollinators can include native bees, butterflies, moths, and others. Earlier-blooming flowers are especially appreciated by native bees. They are active earlier in the season than the well-known honeybee. A standout bee favorite second only to bachelor buttons is the pincushion flower. Our patch is so full of active bees that we must harvest before 10 a.m. just to get into the patch without causing a stir.

The beneficial insects working hard in our gardens include: bees, hoverflies, ground beetles, spiders, wasps, soldier beetles, ladybugs, damsel bugs, big-eyed bug, assassin bug, and many others. While some of these may seem creepy to the faint of heart, their contribution to pest control has taught me to

Some of the beneficial insects living in our gardens. 1.The valuable native pollinator long-horned bees on black-eyed Susans, one of their favorite crops; 2. Black swallowtail caterpillar on *Ammi majus*; 3. Ladybug nymph eating aphids and adults mating; 4. Bumblebee visiting a tender annual *Gomphocarpus physocarpus* flower.

appreciate them for what they do and to let go of my fear. I was terrified of paper wasps until I witnessed one of them snatching a large caterpillar from a flower and flying off with its prize. Wow, nature's pest control in action! I have since learned that wasps don't want to sting me – they want my bad bugs. Now I happily roll out the red carpet for them.

Once you learn a little about who the good guys are, what they need, and how they operate in your garden, you will be fascinated. One of my favorites is the hoverfly (or flower fly), which actually looks like a bee. I call them our search-and-destroyers of aphids. They have super flying abilities so they can hover over flowers searching for aphid colonies. When they find them, they lay one single transparent egg that hatches in just a few days. That single larva will consume hundreds of aphids. What could be easier than that?

What do beneficial insects need? They need a garden that is totally free from all pesticides, herbicides and other chemicals. They need plants that provide nectar, pollen, and habitat. You don't have to purchase beneficial insects, because if you plant what they like, they will come on their own. In fact, most gardens already have a few – they just need some encouragement to grow into a larger community. If these guys discover what they need in your garden, they will stay and reproduce. You will have an amazing work force. Beneficial insects are at the root of my success with organic pest prevention and control on my farm.

Once you begin to attract these guys to the garden you will need to know who they are. It is essential that you become a stellar bug identifier so you know the difference between good bugs and bad bugs. An easy-to-use book is *Good Bug Bad Bug*, by Jessica Walliser. In addition to having great photos of adults and larvae to help you identify them, it gives good advice on ways to attract or remove said bugs.

Make sure you have continuous blooms throughout the season so your good garden workers will stay on the job. Don't be alarmed at the presence of some bad bugs – the good bugs have to have something to eat! With their early blooms, hardy annuals will give the garden a head start on building a diverse community of beneficial insects. The hardy annual group includes some of the richest nectar flowers, which will keep your bugs happy there in your garden for the whole season.

Birds Benefit the Garden

Birds are excellent consumers of insects. The spring garden is of special value to them because many are raising a brood of hungry babies. The way our birds go after insects, spring pests hardly have a chance to get a foothold in our garden. Did you know that hummingbirds eat aphids as a source of protein? Wrens often have large broods of babies and are constantly on the hunt for insects to provide for themselves and their babies. And even the robin – while it's searching for its favorite (the earthworm) it snacks on insects it spots along the way. All this adds up to a lot of bugs being eating by these beautiful workers. Pest control for free!

The prodigious insect consumption is just an added bonus in my garden. Best of all is being surrounded by these birds – seeing their beautiful colors and graceful shapes, hearing their songs and watching them court and hunt. We have Eastern bluebirds here that follow us around the garden. They are amazing hunters. When they have babies, the male is constantly bringing insects to the house for the mom and little ones. I can hardly see how he finds enough. It is no wonder that birds are few and

The nymphs of the leaf-footed bug are frequently eaten by our garden birds. This bug causes similar damage as the stink bug with its piercing sucking mouth parts.

far between in gardens where pesticides and other chemicals are used – all of their food sources have been eliminated. Nothing puts a grin on my face faster than seeing a young bluebird flutter his helpless baby wings while sitting on the fence line, his mom poking one of our garden bugs down his throat. Life is really good in a spring garden.

Water. To keep this feathered crew on the job, we go out of our way to provide what they need in our garden. In addition to not using any chemicals, an easy way to encourage bird visitors is to have water readily available. Birds need water not only to drink, but also for bathing, which helps them stay in top flying condition.

To encourage creatures beneficial to the garden:

- Grow hardy annuals.
- Do not use any pesticides, herbicides or other chemical in the garden.
- Mulch the garden to provide a moist environment that offers hiding places for spiders, beetles, frogs, and others.

- Provide a water source and they will gather there. I like to use an upside-down outdoor trash can lid that has several large flat rocks in it. Fill so the water does not cover the rocks. Birds and insects will land on the rocks and walk down to the water's edge. I fill my water sources daily.
- Plant large masses of the same plant; this allows beneficial insects to find them more easily.
- Plan to have blooms available from early spring until frost.
- Provide perches in the garden to draw visitors. The stakes we use for the flower support netting are in hot demand. Assorted birds and dragonflies take turns sitting on them all season long.

❧ Reap the Rewards in Your Garden ❧

Every garden is full of rewards – you just have to go out, watch, and listen. Once you've shared flowers from your abundance or seen a proud mother bird feeding her precious babies on the garden fence, you will never want to miss spring in a garden.

Ten

GETTING THE MOST AND LETTING GO

Living in one season while planning and planting for the next – that sums up my gardening life. What this means is that at the same time as I am consumed by the spring-blooming hardy-annual garden – harvesting and tending – I am also planning and planting my summer garden. I'm living in the heat of summer-loving zinnias and sunflowers, and I'm working on the fall and next spring garden. This rhythm is what holds my interest and brings me hope. If I have a flop for whatever reason – operator error, weather, or a life catastrophe – my hope lies in the next season that is just around the corner. This is the secret to my chronic optimism. It has made me a better gardener and a successful farmer.

Snapdragons, feverfew, and *Ammi visnaga* are joined by tender summer annuals zinnias and Celosia cockscomb, to make an early summer bouquet.

During the charming days of spring, keep your eye on summer and all the promise she holds. The spring garden will slowly diminish, allowing you to turn your attention from snapdragons and sweet peas to the beauties of summer. It is the fleeting nature of a seasonal garden that allows you to be sad when a season is over, but happy to welcome the next one springing forth.

❧ Getting the Most ❧

It is natural to be in the garden more in springtime than any other time of the year, emerging from what may have been a long winter into bright sunshine, pleasant conditions and plants growing and making buds. The pleasure of being outside lends itself to getting the most out of your plants. Here are the steps to follow to give the garden what it needs in order to produce the most.

- Complete any needed thinning of direct-sown or self-sown seedlings. While immature seedlings may look healthy when crowded, they will not continue to look good or be healthy when mature.

- Early spring is the best time to transplant any self-sown seedlings, while they're still small.

- Plants will quickly grow to full height. If you plan to use it, install flower support before they start to shoot up. For a more natural look, try using stakes or saplings for support. Create a supportive web by going from stake to stake with garden twine. When installed early in the season, flower support netting disappears as the plants grow through it. A late installation of either of these rarely goes well or looks good.

- Make a weekly habit of going to the garden with a tub of mulch and a hoe in tow. Pull or hoe any weeds and then top off that area with more mulch.

- Feed plants with liquid organic fertilizer according to instructions. This can be a drench, which is poured on the soil, or it can be a foliar feeding, which is sprinkled or sprayed on the foliage.

- Once blooming begins in the cutting garden, establish the habit of harvesting all of the flowers that are ready a couple of times a week. For a landscape, begin weekly removal of fading blooms that no longer contribute color. See Chapter 5 for where to make the cuts for specific flowers.

- Place a birdbath in the garden to attract birds for insect control. Place a large rock or two in the bath for young birds, butterflies and good bugs to land on. Fill with fresh water daily.

As these plants move into summer, some will keep up the good work while others get tired. Cutting old blooms and foliage can revive and stimulate new growth.

Enjoy the garden and flowers!

A birdbath in your garden will attract types of birds that eat insects but don't frequent feeders. Providing cover and a perch is also appreciated by our feathered friends.

❧ Letting Go ❧

As summer arrives, some of the earliest bloomers begin to lose their luster while others are still going strong. When this is the case, cut those that are problematic to within 2 inches of ground level. This will eliminate the eyesore from the garden, and it just might encourage them to regrow nice foliage and bloom again. Many of these flowers will continue to bloom into late summer, although not always with the quality or quantity of their spring blooms.

Larkspur flowers past their peak for harvesting as a cut flower but still putting on a show in the landscape. Leaving the flowers in the garden to develop seed will allow them to self-sow for next year's flowers.

Each summer, after weeks of harvesting, our cutting garden snapdragons begin to decline, and I have to make a choice. Attempt to revive or remove? The bed looks great at a distance, but when you go to harvest, you find that the stems are too short to be of use as a cut flower, which is the purpose of this garden. If this were a landscape bed, I'd be pleased to keep up the regular deadheading and continue to enjoy beautiful blooms on shorter stems. My choice for that cutting garden, however, is to pull the snapdragons out and prepare for the next crop.

Overcoming the fear or reluctance to cut back or remove plants will transform you and your garden. This is another lesson learned from my garden. There are far too many good things to enjoy in the garden to waste time fretting over a worn-out plant. It is OK to enjoy a plant for a time, and then let it go! Once I realized that, gardening became a whole lot more fun and rewarding.

⁑ Anyone for Fall Blooms? ⁂

For regions with cooler summers, hardy annual plants can be maintained through summer for a repeat performance come fall. However, there are many regions with hot and humid summers that bring hardy annual plants to their demise. A mid-to-late summer planting of hardy annuals can bring on a fresh crop of flowers as fall comes on and heads into winter.

Dahlias are perfect garden and bouquet companions to fall blooming hardy annuals.

My favorite plants to start indoors during early summer for fall blooming are ornamental kales, snapdragons, pansies, and sweet William (all 100-120 days from seed to maturity). They provide great garden color as well as cut flowers. They tolerate cold weather well and often bloom in our garden beyond Thanksgiving.

Tips for fall blooms:

- Select plants that are able to bloom in the fall even as the day lengths begin to shorten.

- To know when to start your seeds, count back from your first fall frost date the number of days required for the plant to mature and bloom. I add days to this time to have more blooming time.

- Start transplants of kale, snapdragons, pansies, and sweet William indoors in cool conditions.

- It is ideal to grow these plants a little longer as a transplant before planting in the garden. This allows you to provide cooler conditions as needed, such as being able to relocate containers on a hot day into shade.

- Be sure to provide the nutrition your plants need to mature and bloom.

This fall-blooming garden will start life in warmer conditions and grow into its more desirable cool weather conditions. These plants will begin to thrive and bloom as fall comes on. The nighttime temperatures drop, but the days are still bright and warm. There are some great fall-blooming companions to plant that are not in the hardy annual family: cosmos, dahlias, and 'Pro-cut' sunflowers (Pro-cut is a variety of sunflowers that are day-length neutral.) Your fall garden can be full of fresh blossoms when you ponder the possibilities in summer and go for it.

Encourage Reseeding

Many hardy annuals will self-sow their seeds in the garden. This wonderful process means that you may not have to replant seeds again for many years, but you will need to offer a little encouragement and management. Some hardy annual flowers are more apt at doing this than others. Those overachievers are easily controlled with a hoe or by eliminating the flowers before they make and scatter seed.

To allow plants to develop seeds, the flowers must remain on the plant so that it can go on to make seeds. Once the flower head dries and cracks or bursts open, the ripe seeds are ready to cast themselves in the garden. The seeds can be left to their own accord to scatter in the garden. You can collect some of the heads to scatter elsewhere in the garden. An excellent and inexpensive gift for a gardening friend is to share the seed heads from flowers you grew. Write sowing instructions on a paper lunch bag, gather the ripe seed heads and place in the bag. Tie a ribbon around the bag and share.

If you have a cutting garden you can still encourage reseeding. Choose two to three of the plants to be the seed producers, preferably strong growers with nice blooms. Stop harvesting from these plants. Continue to harvest cut flowers from the rest. To tag the seed producing plants, cut a white plastic bag into 2x12-inch strips. Tie the strip on the plants to be skipped over in harvest.

To control self-seeding or to be selective as to which plants you allow to self-sow, remove flowers from those you don't want to develop seeds. I find this works to control certain colors in a mix that are stronger self-sowers than some other colors in the mix. Mixed-color larkspur is a great example. In my garden, dark pink dominates in reseeding; after a couple of years, there are no other colors. To encourage the survival of other colors, I remove the flowers of most of the dark pink when the patch begins to fade. This seems to even the playing field, and I get more of a variety of colors reseeding.

Love-in-a-mist pods, which develop following the flower. Each pod is full of seeds that once ripe will burst and scatter seeds.

Planting seeds directly in the garden in the straightest rows possible will make hoeing chores much easier.

As the season of blooms come to an end for your hardy annual flowers, take a minute to jot down some notes on your calendar of lessons learned. Because I use last year's calendar to plan this year's garden, I like to go back and write notes on the month I actually planted that specific plant. This gathers all my information in the spot I am going to look to when I begin planning. Because many of the chores related to hardy annual gardening are off the timeline of our "before hardy annuals" gardening calendar, it will take time and these little reminders to create new natural habits.

Plant markers. My most recent lesson learned is just how important it is to plant seeds in the garden in a pattern that is identified with plant markers. This becomes very obvious when the weekly hoeing chore is skipped a couple of times (it happens to all of us) and the weeds are sprouting and growing along with your flower seedlings. Who can tell the difference between flowers or weed seedlings? Planting in a pattern that is marked with plant ID markers is essential to easy maintenance. This makes hoeing chores very simple because you know exactly where to avoid hoeing to protect seedlings. My calendar now has "straight rows" written on the months we plant seeds directly in the garden. This reminder will help me to think of the job to come and how difficult it can be when the rows wander about and are not marked.

❦ Keep Trying ❦

With each passing year I continue to learn from my successes and mistakes. I add more flowers to my try-to-grow list because I now know it's often been my timing of when to plant that hindered success. When timing is coupled with great growing conditions, the results are inspiring!

Enjoy the season you are living in and be liberated to let go and move on. It is the next natural step in a garden.

Canterbury Bells 'Champion'

Appendix A

USDA Plant Hardiness Zone Map

You can easily find the plant hardiness for any area of the U.S. by entering your zip code at:
http://planthardiness.ars.usda.gov/PHZMWeb/

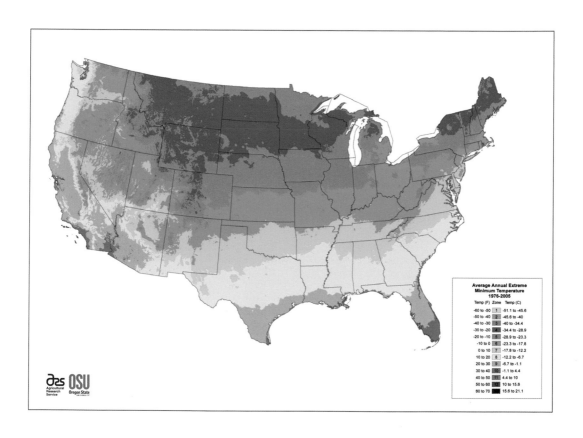

Appendix B

BOTANICAL NAME	COMMON NAMES	WINTER HARDINESS ZONE	SEED STARTING METHOD (Preferred method listed first)
Agrostemma githago	Corn Cockle	7	Sow outdoors
Ammi majus	Bishop's Flower, Queen Anne's Lace	7	Sow indoors; sow outdoors
Ammi visnaga	Green Mist	7	Sow outdoors; sow indoors
Anchusa azurea	Dropmore, Bugloss (Blue and Italian)	3	Sow indoors; sow outdoors
Anethum graveolens	Dill	8	Sow outdoors; sow indoors
Antirrhinum majus	Snapdragons	4 – varieties may vary	Sow indoors
Brassica oleracea	Ornamental Kale	7	Sow indoors
Bupleurum griffithii	Bupleurum	5	Sow outdoors
Calendula officinalis	Pot Marigold, Calendula	7	Sow indoors; sow outdoors
Campanula medium	Canterbury Bells, Bellflower	5	Sow indoors
Centaurea cyanus	Bachelor Button, Cornflower	6	Sow outdoors
Daucus carota var. sativus	False Queen Anne's Lace	7	Sow indoors; sow outdoors
Delphinium	Delphinium	3	Sow indoors
Delphinium consolida	Larkspur	6	Sow outdoors
Dianthus barbatus	Sweet William	5	Sow indoors
Digitalis purpurea	Foxglove, Lady's Glove	5	Sow indoors; sow outdoors
Eustoma	Lisianthus	7	Sow indoors
Godetia	Godetia, Farewell-to-Spring	8	Sow indoors; sow outdoors
Helichrysum bracteatum	Strawflower	8	Sow indoors; sow outdoors
Lathyrus odoratus	Sweet Peas	7	Sow indoors; sow outdoors
Moluccella laevis	Bells of Ireland	7	Sow outdoors; sow indoors
Monarda hybrida	Lambada	7	Sow indoors; sow outdoors
Nigella	Love-in-a-Mist	6	Sow outdoors
Orlaya grandiflora	White Lace Flower	6	Sow indoors; sow outdoors
Papaver nudicaule	Iceland Poppy	6	Sow outdoors
Rudbeckia hirta	Black-Eyed Susan	5	Sow indoors; sow outdoors
Scabiosa atropurpurea	Pincushion Flower	7	Sow indoors; sow outdoors
Tanacetum parthenium	Feverfew	5	Sow indoors; sow outdoors
Trachelium caeruleum	Throatwort	7	Sow indoors
Viola x wittrockiana	Pansy	7	Sow indoors

Appendix C

Information and Recommendations for Tools, Supplies & Seeds

Floating row cover: This is a lightweight fabric that provides protection from cold, wind, insect pressure, deer, rabbits and squirrels. It also helps to retain moisture in newly planted seed beds between waterings. Available in several weights, I use the AG-19 version that allows 85% of air, water and light to pass through it and it provides 4 degrees of temperature protection. When more cold protection is desired, I place two layers of fabric on the bed. Use heavy objects such as rocks or gallon jugs full of water to hold in place. Cover is reusable from year to year when stored out of weather between uses. "Floating" indicates that the fabric is lightweight enough to rest directly on the plants and no support hoops required. Support hoops, as described on page 141, can be used to optimize and expand the uses of a floating row cover.

Support netting: This is plastic netting that is suspended over the flower planting using stakes to provide support during rain and wind. The netting has 6x6-inch openings that allow flowers to grow up through it, making it almost invisible once plants are mature. The desired height of the netting is half of the mature height of a given plant. (Example: For a 36-inch-tall flower at maturity, netting should be at 18 inches. Install on planting after mulching is complete but while plants are still shorter than half of their mature height. Netting is only as strong as the stakes used to hold it up; 48-60-inch metal U-channel fence posts do well, driven into the soil so the wings on the foot of the post are below soil level.

To install: roll netting out over the planting, drive a stake through the end corner squares, pulling netting snug from side-to-side but not overly tight. Go to the other end of the planting, pull the netting snug and place end stakes. Place stakes opposite one another on both sides of netting every 8 feet or closer. I place old tennis balls with a slit on the tops of the posts, once installed, to prevent scratches and impalings while tending the garden. U-channel posts are available at your local building supply store. Post removal tip: fence post pullers are available for easy post removal at season end. Found at local farm and horse supply stores.

Support Hoops: These are used for lifting the floating row cover off of the surface of the planting. The increased air space creates an excellent growing environment that is favorable for any number of longer term uses. I leave covers on beds throughout our winters for wind and deer protection until it is time to install support netting. During summer, hooped uses include providing better ventilation and protection from pests. Hoop length depends on the width of your bed. The height of the installed hoop is approximately 18-24 inches from ground level, with 8-12 inches of hoop pushed into the soil. Hoops are available ready-made from Johnny's (listed below) or you can make your own using pex ½-inch pipe or #9 wire available where plumbing and building supplies are sold.

Seeds: When you buy from retailers that are in the gardening trade and practice proper seed handling and storage prior to your purchase, it is a safeguard that the seeds are alive when you purchase them. After purchase, most seeds can be stored for more than one year; however, the rate of germination will diminish over time. Proper storage of seeds includes low humidity and cool temperatures.

Tools:

Hoes for weeding: What sets the hand and stand-up hoes apart from others is the angle of the blade to the ground which makes them effortless and efficient to use to remove weeds of all sizes. The hand tool is called the *Japanese hand hoe* and the stand-up version, a *trapezoid garden hoe*. Both allow you to use like a razor to glide through the top 1-2 inches of soil, eliminating germinating and young weeds while not bringing up fresh soil from deeper down that is full of more weed seeds.

Cut-Flower shears: The qualities I look for in shears for harvesting cut flowers and deadheading flowers are a small, lightweight tool that has bypass blades that can be sharpened and that lasts more than a season. The Saboten shear is a small and lightweight shear that is easy on the arms and hands.

Cut-flower food: To increase the vase life of fresh cut flowers use cut-flower food. Our clean harvest buckets are filled with water and a dose of fresh cut-flower food according to directions. It helps to keep the water clean, provide nutrients to the stems for greener foliage and to encourage continued bud development and prevent clogged stems. It makes such a difference that we include in each of our bouquets a large packet of food for the customer to use at home. Read the instructions for the volume of water to mix with your packet.

Organic fertilizers: I consider my flowers as athletes. I demand top quality abundance from them, so I must provide what they need to produce it. There are many excellent organic fertilizers in dry and liquid forms widely available. We use a dry fertilizer when preparing the soil before planting and a liquid fertilizer throughout the growing season, applied as a soil drench (pour on soil) and foliar feeding (sprinkled or sprayed on foliage). What guides me in my selection is that it is OMRI certified (Organic Materials Review Institute) and is based on sustainable ingredients such as fish, seaweed, and processed animal manures. When applied according to directions you get a longer season of bloom and more abundance.

Seed-starting supplies: I use the Micro 20-size blocker almost exclusively, and the 2-inch blocker only when seeds are too large for the smaller blocker (sweet peas, pot marigolds, etc.) In addition to the tools and supplies for soil blocking available, the companies listed on the next page also provide online videos and DVDs on how to start seeds with soil blocking. The blocking mix recipe is included in Chapter 6 and is also available ready-made from the listed sources. Once equipped with the soil blocking seed-starting gear, you just add blocking mix and seeds in the coming years.

Biodegradable mulch film: This is especially useful for a working garden when you're not placing organic mulch such as bark or straw on top of it. The Bio Telo brand is made of Mater-Bi®, a non-GMO corn starch-based raw material. Planting through film with or without an organic mulch topper is easy by punching a hole with your finger or sharp tool. The film can be used independently for its soil warming and weed suppressing qualities. It can also be turned into the soil at season's end.

Sources for Tools, Supplies and Seeds:

The Gardener's Workshop
www.thegardenersworkshop.com
888.977.7159

This is my company. TGW specializes in everything cut-flowers – seeds, gardening and flower arranging tools and supplies. We offer educational programs nationally.

Johnny's Selected Seeds
www.johnnyseeds.com
877.564.6697

Offers tools, supplies and seeds.

Peaceful Valley
www.groworganic.com
888.784.1722.

Offers tools, supplies and seeds.

Bachelor Buttons 'Pinkie

Books of Interest

The Easy Cut-Flower Garden, Lisa Mason Ziegler, The Gardener's Workshop, 2011

The Flower Farmer, Lynn Byczynski, Chelsea Green, 2008 (2nd edition; my own dog-eared copy is the earlier, 1997 edition)

Good Bug, Bad Bug, Jessica Walliser, St. Lynn's Press, 2011

Grow Organic, Doug Oster and Jessica Walliser, St. Lynn's Press, 2007

Local Color: Growing Specialty Cut Flowers, Frank and Pamela Arnosky, Fairplain Publications, 2010

The New Organic Grower, Eliot Coleman, Chelsea Green, 1995

Specialty Cut Flowers, Allan Armitage and Judy Laushman, Timber Press, 2008

Links of Interest

www.ascfg.org
Association of Specialty Cut Flower Growers

www.slowflowers.com
Connecting consumers with floral professionals who use American-grown flowers.

Acknowledgments

Cool Flowers would have never come to pass if it had not been for one who believed in me and what I have to say. Susan Yoder Ackerman tended and cultivated my career as a writer; without her encouragement, I would have never pursued the written word. Our paths crossed through friendship and the love of gardening and grew into a working relationship of mentor and student. Her gift of storytelling shines through in my writing. Susan, you have given one of the greatest gifts I have received. Thank you.

The warm welcome I received from St. Lynn's Press made the journey of writing *Cool Flowers* a joy. Paul Kelly showed confidence in my story and provided the wonderful support staff to make it all come true. Cathy Dees held my hand and offered such amazing advice that my fears were dashed and my confidence soared. Holly Rosborough took my words and Suzanne's photographs to bring this amazing book to life. Paul, Cathy, and Holly – thank you ever so much for making my dream come true.

Many others have contributed to this rich gardening life I live – some through their life's work that led to books that opened doors for me and others having a more personal hand; all worked together for my gardening good. I am often asked how I got started and the answer is always the same: I read a book. The three books that blazed the path for me to charge down: *The Flower Farmer*, by Lynn Byczynski, *We're Gonna Be Rich!* by Frank and Pamela Arnosky, and *The New Organic Grower*, by Eliot Coleman. Lynn, Frank and Pamela have become friends over the years and I have received even more wisdom beyond their books – all three are rock stars in the flower farming industry. I thank them all for taking the time to put their wisdom on paper for the rest of us to learn. And special thanks to Eliot Coleman – I have enjoyed and absorbed so much from the pages of his books. He has taught me how an organic garden works and the secrets to seed starting using soil blocking. My organic gardening success is deeply rooted in his methods.

Joining with like-minded people has developed me into the flower grower I am today. The Association of Specialty Cut Flower Growers provides flower farmers an opportunity to come together to learn and further the local flower movement. I thank those farmers that came before me to get it all started and those that serve now; they have made me a better farmer, gardener, and business owner.

The results of all my gardening ambitions have been welcomed and supported by the local floral industry. My very first commercial customer, Eddie Sturgill at Anderson's Home and Garden Showplace, took me under his wing and taught me the ropes of the floral industry. The following year I expanded and added Williamsburg Floral, Seasons of Williamsburg, Colonial Williamsburg, The Flower Cupboard, Events in Bloom, and Jeff's Flowers Of Course. These first customers warmly embraced me long before "local" was a buzz word, and their continued kindness encourages me beyond what they will ever imagine.

I would have nothing to write or speak about without my sister, Suzanne Mason Frye. She has been in the trenches with me since my beginning while bringing it all to life with her photographs. My friend Bobo Smith has stood alongside us growing, cutting, and wilting in the heat – thank you both for loving this crazy flower farming thing as much as me!

Most of all, thanks be to God, my husband, Steve, and Dad, who guide and support me daily in growing and sharing my love of a garden.

Corn Cockle 'Ocean Pearl'

About the Author

Lisa Mason Ziegler is a commercial cut-flower grower, author, and accomplished speaker. Lisa tells it all when it comes to gardening, cut flowers, and doing it organically and sustainably. Lisa's experiences have been gathered from everyday life on her cut-flower farm nestled in the midst of the city of Newport News, Virginia. In the farm's blooming season, from May until October, it produces over 10,000 stems of flowers per week.

Early in her farming career, it became clear that perhaps her strongest gift is sharing her passion and knowledge of gardening with others. She began speaking to local interested groups in 2002 and now has reached hundreds of groups, from New York to Texas. In 2005, the next natural step was to launch an online garden shop – The Gardener's Workshop – offering the gardening tools, supplies and seeds that are used on the farm. The Gardener's Workshop continues to grow and educate gardeners.

Visit www.lisaziegler.com and www.thegardenersworkshop.com for more.

Other books from St. Lynn's Press:

Slow Flowers
by Debra Prinzing
144 pages, Hardback
ISBN: 978-0-9832726-8-7

Fine Foliage
by Karen Chapman & Christina Salwitz
160 pages, Hardback
ISBN: 978-0-9855622-2-9

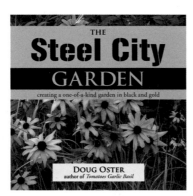

The Steel City Garden
by Doug Oster
176 pages, Hardback
ISBN: 978-0-9855622-3-6

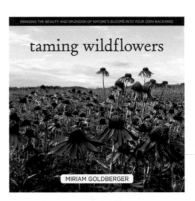

Taming Wildflowers
by Miriam Goldberger
208 pages, Hardback
ISBN: 978-0-9855622-6-7